# THE
# PRACTICAL
# SIDE OF
# REINCARNATION

# THE PRACTICAL SID
# REINCAR

OF

# NATION

David Graham
Introduction by Brad Steiger

Prentice-Hall, Inc., Englewood Cliffs, N.J.

*The Practical Side of Reincarnation*
by David Graham
Copyright © 1976 by Other Dimensions, Inc.
All rights reserved. No part of this book may be
reproduced in any form or by any means, except
for the inclusion of brief quotations in a review,
without permission in writing from the publisher.
Printed in the United States of America
Prentice-Hall International, Inc., London
Prentice-Hall of Australia, Pty. Ltd., Sydney
Prentice-Hall of Canada, Ltd., Toronto
Prentice-Hall of India Private Ltd., New Delhi
Prentice-Hall of Japan, Inc., Tokyo

10 9 8 7 6 5 4 3 2 1

Library of Congress Cataloging in Publication Data
Graham, David,
    The practical side of reincarnation.
    Includes index.
    1. Reincarnation. I. Title.
BL515.G67 1976    129'.4    76-2603
ISBN 0-13-693903-1

# Introduction by Brad Steiger

In 1968 a young woman with long blonde hair called on me in the hope that she might be employed as my secretary. At that time, my daughter Julie was three years old—quiet, and painfully shy with anyone outside the family. Those who were even slightly less than really close friends would make Julie clam up and withdraw.

Julie took one look at the young woman, and her face erupted in a broad smile. She spread wide her arms and ran giggling across the floor to throw herself in a hard embrace about the body of the stranger. "I *liked* it when you were my mommy," Julie said, smiling warmly up at the young woman.

Yes, I hired Jeanyne. She was my secretary for five years, and she remains a close and dear friend of the family. But could she really have been Julie's mother in some past life? Or was that merely childish babble? What could possibly have caused my daughter to run and embrace a total stranger? And, at a time when her own mother was the center of her universe, what could have prompted Julie to bestow that coveted position upon a young blonde woman whom she had never seen before?

Whether we can accept the thesis of reincarnation depends, I suppose, upon the limits we set upon consciousness and upon the premise that there is within man some spiritual essence which somehow survives physical death. Twenty years as a psychic investigator have convinced me that the perimeters of consciousness are limitless; and it seems to me I have always believed that man is more than a physical thing.

I remember as a child that my favorite hymn—and the one I always requested when it was my turn to choose for religion class—was the one that began: "I'm but a stranger here, Heaven is my home." I have always been troubled—even when

I was a rigid child of orthodoxy—by memories and associations which certainly were not my own. Since I was reared on an Iowa farm, tutored in a small village high school, and spiritually nurtured by the Evangelical Lutheran Church, my range of experiences were decidedly limited. Yet I had a "knowing" and a "remembering" of people, places, and things obviously beyond my ken. Although this knowledge brought me good grades and a reputation for being considerably brighter than I probably was, this awareness caused me no end of private turmoil and endless dark nights of the soul.

For reasons I'll explain later, I write my books under the name of Brad Steiger. From time to time, earnest literary detectives confront me with what they apparently consider some remarkable bit of deduction: "Is your *real* name Eugene Olson?" they ask, often accusingly, as if the name under which I have written 50 books is somehow unreal. I can only answer that Brad Steiger is my *real* name. Eugene Olson is my tribal name, but also *real. Hat-yas-swass* is my adoptive Seneca name, and it is also a *real* name.

Although I have always loved my parents dearly and, through them, was blessed with the happiest of childhoods, I have always felt uncomfortable with the name they gave me. The name with which I was christened, Eugene Olson, is a perfectly fine name; but I have never really vibrated with it as if it were right for me. I have a vivid memory of weeping, surrounded by amused adults, as I tried to explain that the name they were calling me was not my real name.

As a boy growing up on the corn-seeded prairies of Iowa, I continually envisioned myself walking among thick stands of trees, hilly trails, sparkling streams. I seemed not to be a child of Scandinavian-American extraction, but an American Indian. When I grew older, my reading synchronized with my "memory" and I recognized the New England states as my "home."

Until we settled in Decorah, Iowa, which is like a slice of transplanted Vermont/New Hampshire/Upstate New York, I had felt geographically misplaced. Recently when my wife Marilyn and I were adopted into the Wolf Clan of the Seneca on the Cattaraugus Reservation near Buffalo, New York, I felt very much as though a part of me had truly come home. The Medicine People there agreed with me in stating that I had truly walked those trails before.

I have a great terror of the sea, and I have no yearnings for an ocean voyage. Long before the book and movie *Jaws* regenerated atavistic fears in many of us, I had a vivid "memory" of a storm-ravaged sea, a crash of a vessel against jutting rocks, and a violent, horrible death at the jaw of a great marine eating-machine.

Whenever I pull on my boots (I never wear shoes), I have a peculiar mental "rush"—strangely gratifying, yet frustrating in its too-rapid montage of memories-data-scenes-people. Virtually the identical "rush" occurs whenever I light or (especially strong) blow out a candle. I "feel" Spain. I am walking down a long corridor, flanked on either side by somber men. There is a large door ahead of us. We pause before the door, and it begins to open. Flash to riding hard on horseback. Rapid flash to vivid montage of faces and places which all "feel" like Spain.

Although I no longer profess the parochial religion of my childhood, I still acknowledge mankind's spirituality and celebrate the assertion that the only lasting truths are the soul, imagination, and inspiration. The intuitive feeling that I am one with all others and that we are individually and collectively more nonphysical than physical entities has become intensified by both study and personal experience.

But believing in life after death is not necessarily synonymous with a belief in reincarnation. To say that the essential self within man survives physical death is not to say that that same essence awakens within a new physical body. The cautious will say there may be alternate explanations. If the perimeters of consciousness are limitless, then there may be any number of means whereby information—ostensible "memories" — might be received on some level of awareness.

I quite agree that there may be alternate explanations for experiences, memories, and situations suggestive of reincarnation. I have spent a number of years researching a good many of mine. One might interpret them as bits of old movies stuck in my childhood's subconscious, fragments of others' dramatized creativity stubbornly adhering to my own creative processes, early reading experiences somehow fastened to my psyche in a melding of pseudo-experience. But there is a decidedly different feeling about the "memories" that I experienced. They seem so much more than daydreams grown independent, remembered incidents clutching for sustained imagery, or the product of resourceful levels of imagination. Perhaps it has something to do with the modalities of consciousness which each aspect of the soul may choose for itself. At this point within my own thought, I must state that I believe reincarnation may be *one* of the forms which survival takes.

Others of these peculiar "memories" have returned to haunt me with the important questions they suggest. Like the American Indian consciousness, the terrible death scene at sea, and the Spanish fragments, they are relatively incomplete and do not provide me with a great deal of information. One of them, however, dramatically altered my life and provided the one most persistent and disturbing element in my dream dramas of youth. It also serves to illustrate the "practical" aspect of reincarnation which my friend David Graham has chosen as his theme for this book. How else does one explain such an instance as the following?

As early as I can remember, I periodically suffered a terrible dream of being high in the air, momentarily engulfed in a blast of noise and flame, then falling through space. As a child, I suffered from acrophobia, a gut-wrenching, sweat-popping fear of heights. Being tossed in the air by my six-foot-four uncle was a terrifying experience. Climbing trees and swinging from branches was out of the question. Once I did manage to climb a short ladder at a friend's house, but then had to suffer the humiliation of having his mother help me down.

When I was about thirteen, I discovered the marvelous mechanism within dreams which enabled me to control them. I utilized dreams to enable me to have my lessons letter-perfect. I ordered up my fantasy drama before bedtime, then enjoyed my theatre of the psyche. But my control crumbled when, unbidden and always unwelcome, there came that swooping nightmare of exploding into flame and hurtling out into space. I became convinced that I was experiencing a precognitive dream: one day I would die in an aircraft explosion. I vowed to avoid air travel and thus avoid my fate.

When I was in my late teens I experienced a moment of immense pleasure when I suddenly thought of (or remembered) the name that vibrated in greater attunement with a more forceful aspect of myself. So as a twenty-year-old college student Brad Steiger began to write and publish. After teaching high school for six years and college writing courses for four years, and having written a number of books, I had to come to painful grips with my fear of flying. I caused a dilemma for publishers' public relations people. How to arrange a promotional tour for someone who does not fly? I used to hopscotch about the country by commuter trains, buses, and automobile. Sometimes I had to sit up all night on a crowded train, often taking eight hours or more to travel less than 200 miles.

Today I log thousands of miles of air travel each year. And I must attribute the "cure," not to years of psychoanalysis, encounter groups, or any in-vogue therapy, but to the catharsis of the psyche undergoing the death experience in what would appear to be a past life. Although I have always been a history buff and minored in history in college, I have always avoided any study of World War I. Even as a child devouring volume by volume my grandmother's lavish Gustave Doré illustrated *Ridpath's History of the World,* I scarcely opened the volume on the Great War. Whenever I did, I would become extremely restless, my vision would blur, and I would become upset to my stomach. I skipped most class sessions on World War I, but I had no difficulty passing the tests on the unit because it seemed as though I already knew even the minutiae associated with those years of horror.

In my own mind I am certain that I was not dreaming. One night I was awakened to view, as if in a panoramic, Cinema-Scopic vision, a world that had the flavor of northern Europe—specifically Germany—at the turn of the century. Soon, I felt myself bending over a man several years older than I. He was writing at a desk. Judging by his elegant smoking jacket and the furniture in the room, the man was quite wealthy. I knew that I hated him. I knew that he had married the woman I loved. She was a life-long love, a childhood sweetheart who had yielded to parental pressure and married a much older, much better-situated man. The legal barrier did little to prevent our continuing our love affair, however, until I could bear the arrangement no longer.

I became aware of *her* standing there. Her hair was blonde rather than auburn, she was a bit taller and heavier, but I knew that she was somehow Marilyn, my present-life wife. Then I became aware of the heavy fireplace poker in my hand. While the woman (the name Gretchen kept coming to mind) stood and watched in quiet approval, I murdered her husband in an atavistic desire to reclaim that which was rightfully mine. In a hideous montage of gore and violence, I saw myself dismembering the body and affecting a crude cremation in a large furnace. I "saw" myself only when I would pass in front of a mirror or other reflective surface. At all other times, I was literally seeing the events through the eyes of the participant—which I "felt" was somehow the same entity that is myself today.

When I had reduced the corpse to as few charred remains as possible, I meticulously bundled them into packages to dump in the harbor. I left my paramour and set about establishing an alibi for the evening. I went to the theatre, visited a cabaret, and spent the evening with boisterous friends.

The next day I placed the bundles in a picnic basket and got aboard a large boat which provided tours of the harbor. I had vivid thoughts of guilt and perverse accomplishment. Grimly, I pondered what the happy holidayers would think if they knew a murderer sat in their midst. I nearly chuckled aloud at the consternation that would be shown if I should reveal what I had in those packages in my picnic basket.

Once the bundles had been surreptitiously dumped in the ocean and the craft had docked, I telephoned my business partner. I knew then that I was an attorney. I knew also that my partner in that time was a close friend of mine in this life.

Although I attempted to be jocular and explain my unannounced holiday as the result of too much to drink the night before, he immediately cut through my charade and informed me that the newspapers were filled with sensational stories about the disappearance and suspected murder of one of the city's wealthiest and most respected merchants. Police had announced clues which implicated the merchant's wife and a male accomplice. Since my partner was well aware of my affair with the man's wife, he snorted over my protestations of shock and concern, and advised me to stay out of the city.

But I had to see my love, to consult with her, to stand beside her in this time of crisis. I paid no attention to my partner's warning and I returned to the city.

As I neared "Gretchen's" home, I saw a large, black old-time four-door sedan parked in front of the ornate stone steps. A crowd was beginning to gather. The front door of the large house opened, and a police inspector led Gretchen to the car. Two officers immediately behind him pushed back the people who were eager to catch a glimpse of the murderess. Just before she stepped into the car, she paused, tall, regal, cool, and turned to look directly into my eyes. Although her features remained impassive, the communication which passed between us was heavy with love, laden with farewell. She had not—and I knew that she would not—betray me to the authorities.

Tears stung my eyes, and I turned quickly and walked through the gathering crowd. The woman I had loved all my life, for whom I had killed, was now being taken from me. I knew that I would never in life see her again.

There was much more: my fleeing the city after bidding a hurried farewell to my partner; a struggle to assemble a new identity in a new city; the outbreak of World War I, and my enlistment in the German Air Force. I lived for the moment, trying desperately to expiate my sins by taking the lives of others for my country. I attempted to keep sorrowful memories from me by erecting a stockade of transient affairs and lost weekends.

Then came the sunny afternoon when, high above the skies over France, we encountered a group of British aircraft. While diving after my chosen prey, I became aware of a sting in my shoulder. I looked around to see blood spurting. A British plane with twin machine guns was swooping right on my tail. There was an explosion, a violent burst of flame, and I was aware of falling unsupported through space.

Can it be possible that I actually lived in Germany at the turn of the century, that I was killed in aerial combat in World War I? Was my name Steiger in that existence? (I may well have changed names then, too—from Steiger to something else when I enlisted. I know "Brad" was not my first name.) Or did my creative psyche fabricate a marvelously detailed psychodrama to provide me with a catharsis whereby I might travel by air and achieve a much more effective schedule for research, lecturing, and promotional activities?

Perhaps my memory-vision suggestive of reincarnation was my own psyche somehow attuning to the actual life experience of one who lived before in a foreign land in a time before my own. Perhaps, in an altered state of consciousness, I somehow "plugged" into a memory pattern that melded with my own psyche until it seemed as though I had myself had those experiences in another lifetime. But regardless of what interpretation anyone might place upon this personal vision, something extremely practical resulted from the experience: I no longer have a fear of flying. The interpretation I immediately gave to my vision was that I was not fated to die in a mid-air explosion in this life, but that I had *already* died in such an explosion in a previous lifetime. Because of that one flash of creativity or knowledge, a fear that had crippled me from childhood was removed. Since that visionary experience, I can at last sit near the window in a tall building. I can walk up open stair flights.

A creative, albeit intensely practical, facet of my psyche may have provided me with a framework whereby I might remove my fear of flying through an ingenious interior psychodrama. But here is the point: whatever my reincarnation experience might have been in *your* reality construct, it must be conceded that in *my* reality construct it served a most practical reason for having come into realization.

Because of that one insightful, or revelatory, evening, all fear of flying was removed. No white knuckle flights, no cold sweats, no nervous starts at every whir and thump of the aircraft. I relax to the point of taking catnaps. I can say in all honesty that I truly enjoy flying. And there has never been a repetition of those falling dreams.

I cannot *prove* that I was that German pilot who died in a fiery mid-air explosion over the war-torn fields of France, but in this present life, the entity who seemed also to be Marilyn was placed very near to me. She was my cousin who lived two miles down the country road in the small Iowa farm community in which we were both reared. Again, there appeared to be a legal barrier to our union, but in this instance a *deus ex machina* negated my having to resort to violence. Marilyn is my *adopted* cousin. As if to take no chances this time around, I married Marilyn when she was eighteen and I was twenty. Although Marilyn does not share such a memory of a previous

xiii

existence, she confesses freely that since childhood she had felt as one with me and knew we would marry.

Interestingly, even though there were no obvious physical resemblances, I "recognized" several of my friends in this life assuming quite different, though strangely related, occupations and situations in that pre-World War I life. For example, my law partner in that life was plump, bald, and considerably older than I. In this life, he is a businessman, solidly built, with a thick head of hair, and is a few days younger than I. Yet in my vision, the two seemed strangely overlapped, so that I knew they were one.

It is interesting that my college aptitude tests had indicated a proficiency as either a lawyer or a writer. Since everyone knew how impractical it was to consider writing as a career, my counselor argued that I should enter law school. I declined a law scholarship in favor of teaching, so that I might more easily write as an avocation.

Then there is the most intriguing item of the British pilot who shot me down. Now if there really is such a spiritual concept as reincarnation and within that concept there actually is the compensating process known as Karma, then it is perhaps realized in my relationship with David Graham. As David will tell you in this book, he seems to have recall of a life in which he was a British pilot who shot down a German flyer, only to have his own life snuffed out in that same aerial dogfight. *If* it is true that David caused my demise in that alleged prior existence, then it certainly seems a fulfillment of Karmic debt that in this lifetime he has devoted himself to watching over me as my business manager!

I have often heard psychic sensitives assert that many entities being incarnated at this time were gassed in the trenches, mangled by the first mechanized armies, blasted by the first large-scale aerial bombings. According to these contemporary seers, such entities are coming back as pacifists, as men and women with a strong aversion to war, the militaristic mind, the warrior motif. I do know that *I* loathe war and that I will devote this existence to doing everything I can to help all people realize that they can transcend that primitive impulse that leads to inhumanity, bloodshed, and the desecration of that sacred bond that unites all men and women.

My "memory" of a past life, then, must not be relegated to the esoteric realms of ethereal and nonutilitarian mysticism. Whatever else it might have been, it was also practical.

# Contents

# Chapter 1

## An Age-Old Idea Whose Time Has Come

I spent many years as a radio and television journalist, and believe me, this is one of the best jobs in the world to give an individual a certain amount of crust. The average reporter, by the time he is a news director or editor, is a true skeptic, if not a confirmed cynic. He has heard it all from politicians, criminals, police officers, celebrities, and would-be celebrities. He has interviewed the great and near great and reported events of every description from the local D.A.R. meeting to the bloody details of every crime and accident imaginable—details not always permitted on the airwaves of our radio stations. In other words, after a few years, the reporter has "had it." New philosophies bounce off the old pro newsman like the proverbial water off a duck's back. Nothing shocks him.

Perhaps this attitude comes of witnessing wasted lives on an almost daily basis. You see a young man convicted of murder and sent to the gallows or a prison cell for the remainder of his earthly life. You learn of a young child being run down by a speeding car, his life snuffed out. You see one individual devoted to preserving life, a dedication found in every hospital where physicians labor endlessly and surgeons work over a body for hours to preserve that small spark of life, while just down the block a masked gunman is holding up a gas station and kills the attendant for being too slow in handing over the day's receipts.

An irony can sometimes be found when, upon investigation, it is revealed that the dedicated physician is an agnostic, with little or no religious affiliation, while the murderer came from a strict religious family. Strange, indeed, yet it is often the case. You are witness to a thousand and one events that seem so meaningless. Regardless of how crusty you may have become, you still maintain a certain reverence for life, and you find yourself asking, —"why?" Why is life so valuable to some, while it seems to have no value to others? How do you make sense out of it all?

Finally, you begin to put it all together.

Strange as it may seem, many of these same journalists can find a certain credibility to the idea that we have lived before— that reincarnation is one theory that makes sense. Reincarnation, by whatever name it may be given, is the basic belief that the essence of us all not only survives physical death—when the body does indeed return to dust and recycles in Nature— but that same essence has been around for a long time before it spilled into the present body, along with its fears and phobias created long ago in the dim past.

In spite of years of seeing life at its worst, I have come to the conclusion that it all has a purpose in the final analysis. The years have taught me that there has to be some higher purpose to life that can only be accomplished by living more than once. Is it not conceivable to assume that the Creative Force behind all things—spiritual and physical—would be no less conservative of the spiritual essence than it would be of the physical clay we use for a few years and then discard? Science tells us that matter is capable of being converted into other forms of matter or energy. Is the Creative Force—God—less concerned with the spiritual nature of man?

After years of news reporting you develop, like a good detective, a certain degree of "gut feeling." You know, without necessarily knowing why you know, that the idea of rebirth has a degree of reason and logic. If you believe that we have lived before, you will then know that events in the past life of the physician or surgeon may have heavily influenced his choice of profession in this life. For example, it might be found that the healer today was guilty of neglect or even murder in a past life, and his inner being or soul demanded retribution. His Karma indicated that to find peace within, he must serve the principle of cause-and-effect. He must gain a notch on the spiritual evolutionary scale to atone, in this life, for the misdeeds of the past. In order to satisfy his soul's yearning he is devoting his entire being at this time to saving, rather than taking, life.

While the adage holds true that to be "news" it must be different, not all news reporting deals with the negative side of life. There are those who make news who are dedicated humanitarians and give every indication that they are leading lives of complete wholeness and may be near the eventual perfection that rebirth is designed to eventually accomplish.

So much for the good doctor—but what about the criminal

with the "Saturday night special" who left his victim to die in a pool of blood? No, he is not making up for a similar act committed against him long ago, for this would not indicate progress, but a complete backsliding. Part of the overall principle of rebirth is the ability to forgive, not to avenge the wrongs committed against the entity. The robber/murderer in this case is of extremely low spiritual development—an entity on the low rung of the spiritual ladder. Although there may be nothing in his past lives to justify such an act, it is a certainty that if he does not meet a similar fate in this life, he will in a lifetime to come. He has set the pattern into motion and will not escape it. He who lives by the sword will die by the sword, but not necessarily in this lifetime. We cannot escape the Law of Retribution—Karma. The murderer must eventually meet a similar fate. Perhaps the victim was working out a similar Karmic fate.

The idea of reincarnation did not originate in the much discussed "occult boom" of the past few years, nor is it limited to the superstitions of more "primitive" cultures. The question of immortality has been uppermost in the minds of human beings since man first fell out of the tree and started asking, "why?" While most religions dating far into antiquity have taught some form of survival beyond death, the Reincarnationist adds another dimension—life before birth—in the eternal journal of birth, death, and rebirth.

Wicca—the Old Religion—is practiced by many today, under a variety of names, ranging from Witchcraft to Paganism. It is truly an ancient religion, antedating Christianity by hundreds of years. It is a nature religion, with overtones which make it similar in certain respects to Amerindian Medicine and Huna. Western religions, especially the more fundamental varieties, continue to promote the idea that witchcraft is akin to satanism. This could not be farther from the truth, for in reality, witches do not believe in Satan, insisting that the Satan mythos is an invention of the Christian Church.

Doctors Gavin and Yvonne Frost are modern Witches teaching age-old religious truths. They operate the School of Wicca in Salem, Missouri, and have dedicated their lives to eradicating the negativity which has been associated with every mention of the word "witchcraft." They are neither devil-worshippers nor satanists, but merely followers of the age-old pre-Christian path of Wicca Craft, the path of the natural bending and adjustment to circumstances. They acknowledge Jesus as one avatar among many, and regard God as something so far beyond human understanding that it cannot be thought about.

I first met Gavin and Yvonne Frost when they visited Decorah a couple years ago. Knowing their basic belief in the concepts of rebirth established in the Wiccan religion, I thought it would add substantially to this book if I could get them to add their comments on the subject:

"It would be comfortable if we could flatly say that prehistoric peoples believed in reincarnation. But it is fairly clear from boat burials and from barrow graves that Indo-European peoples shared with Egyptians a belief in an afterworld where existence was similar to that known here, where dead spirits required a wide range of goods and many servants. These funerary rites and grave goods also tended to indicate a belief in the final resurrection of the actual physical body and hence the need to preserve the earth-plane shell. The brief change to cremation in the Urn Field Cultures can tentatively be interpreted as indicating a dramatic change of philosophy and may, as in the Eastern case, which retained cremation, indicate a belief in reincarnation. We can say that the propitiation of spirits—both animal and human—indicates a high-level understanding of the spirit-and-shell concept, though little belief in reincarnation or transmigration is detectable.

"There is some evidence for a belief in reincarnation in various extant books from Ireland and Wales. The prevalence of 'I have beens' in the Triads seems to us a clear indication of such beliefs."

> *I have been in many shapes,*
> *Before I attained a congenial form.*
> *I have been a narrow blade of a sword,*
> *I have been a drop in the air,*
> *I have been a shining star.*

"Despite Robert Graves' out-of-hand rejection of a literal interpretation of this type of poem, still we in Celtic Wicca tend to believe that the old Bards were quite capable of including both obvious and hidden meanings in their writings. Another source is our own [Celtic] oral and written tradition. This concept of spirit and shell can be seen in the very ancient writings of the *Rig-Veda,* where we read:

> *The Spirit is likened to the Charioteer;*
> *The Body to the Chariot;*
> *And the reins are Wisdom*

"We must also look to Eastern writings for the first thoughts on reincarnation, for the *Bhagavad-Gita* says:

> *As the soul passes in the body*
> *Through childhood, youth, and age,*
> *Even so is its taking on of another body.*

"Soon after this, the Pythagorean and Platonic doctrines of progressive reincarnation swept the Old World. Thus early Christians, especially the followers of Origen, were heavily oriented toward reincarnation, though of what type it is difficult to define. For at the second Council of Constantinople in 553 A.D. it became Christian dogma that reincarnation was heresy, Jesus' atoning sacrifice having broken the cycle for all time. Ever since then, belief in reincarnation has been superfluous and unnecessary to Christians, even though such a belief is clearly indicated in the writings of many famous Christians—for instance, St. Francis of Assisi."

Man has long been told that to see the Kingdom of Heaven he must be perfect, even as his Heavenly Father is perfect. The hallowed halls of churchianity have echoed this theme while failing to maintain the early Christian and ancient teachings of the Hebrews that very specifically underscored the doctrine of rebirth. While most religions echo the theme that we survive physical death, they have eliminated from their canons the very essence of their early teachings that show we have indeed lived before.

If you are one of millions who profess Christianity as your religion, then it is vital to your overall philosophy to know that in Apostolic teachings—prior to 325 A.D.—reincarnation was a very basic part of the doctrine, and it was only a handful of powerful churchmen who overruled this teaching in order to gain unlimited power for themselves. Even the Reformation did not reinstate these truths that would set men free.

"In the thirteenth century," the Frosts continue, "the leader of the Mevlevi Dervishes set down in the *Mathnawi* one of the finest explanations of basic reincarnation theory, which in dramatic terms separates Christian belief from Wiccan."

> *I died as a mineral and became a plant;*
> *I died as a plant and rose to animal;*
> *I died an animal and I was a man.*
> *Why should I fear? When was I less by dying?*
> *Yet once more I shall die as man,*
> *to soar with spirits blest.*
> *But even from this I must pass on:*
> *All except God doth perish.*

> —*Jalalu'l-Din Rumi, 1241 A.D.*

Using the metaphor of the boarding school, the reincarnation system is simple and straightforward. It does not deny anyone his or her individual rights. The spirit is thus its own Akashic Record. It has within itself all the knowledge gained in previous lifetimes in the Boarding School of Life. Its mistakes, blunders, false starts, wild goose chases, abortive efforts, are to be considered as an essential part of the learning experience rather than as "evil" or "sin."

"It is worthwhile here to consider the third-grader who, purely by accident, smashes a dish. We don't consider him to be inherently evil; rather, he lacks experience. So if indeed socially acceptable behavior is one of the goals of his learning process, how irrational it is to believe that antisocial behavior deserves demotion clear back to kindergarten—or to an eternity in the burning sulphurous pit of the principal's office. Such a sentence would serve only to increase the spirit's wish to rebel against the system."

The age-old concepts of the Judeo-Christian community have, by and large, failed to give man a direction and purpose for this life on planet Earth. Not long ago, as we gauge time, the majority of people were satisfied to accept the words of their clergymen concerning life, death, and the hereafter. This has not been so in the latter years of the twentieth century. Today, young and old alike are dissatisfied with the orthodox explanations of life after death, and they can no longer accept the version of the vengeful God who gives little direction to life other than "being good for goodness' sake."

People today are searching as never before for solid answers to age-old questions concerning immortality, direction, and purpose of life.

In *The Seth Material* Jane Roberts asks, "Have you lived before, and will you live again?" and answers this by stating that all of us have been reincarnated and that when we have finished our series of earthly lives, we will continue to exist in other systems of reality. It is, in fact, an idea that has more than crossed the minds of intellectuals since the days of Socrates and before, and today is uppermost in the minds of many highly educated physicians, theologians, astrophysicists, and others not normally considered a part of the metaphysical community.

Is there a practical way to cope with and benefit from this incarnation by using knowledge of past lives? How can such knowledge of past lives help us to solve our daily problems in the material world in which we are presently obligated to live?

If reincarnation cannot serve a practical purpose in our present day-to-day existence here on the tiny mudball we call Earth, then it has no pragmatic value worth wasting time and energy to discuss. It must serve the purpose of making our present incarnation more meaningful, and I believe it does just that.

In a *National Enquirer* interview, actress Karen Black claimed that she can remember at least two past lives. One was in France in the year 1775, when she was married to a man that her wealthy family considered below her class. When her husband was killed, she committed suicide. Still earlier, Miss Black says she remembers being a man who was unfaithful to his wife, but her memories of that life are a bit dimmer.

But what, you may ask, does this have to do with the validity or practicality of the principle of reincarnation?

Miss Black claims that the knowledge of past lives has given her a great advantage in coping with problems of her present incarnation, and that knowing about past incarnations serves as a warning against making the same mistakes this time around. It also gives her a greater satisfaction in the knowledge that she does not have to hurry up and experience everything before she dies.

In a case of hypnotic regression which occurred recently, I witnessed and taped a reverie-state regression of a friend, Steve Yankee, who for some unknown reason had an inborn fear of horses.

Steve was born in a small city in Michigan and had never, until recently, lived on a farm. When he and his wife Luana moved to Decorah last summer, they decided to rent an acreage about seven miles from town. The house is adjacent to a stock farm where the owner has a riding horse. Luana has always liked riding and is an excellent horsewoman, but Steve would not get close to the horse. Yet he was not able to account for his nervousness about the animal.

The irrational fear had actually created no great problem with Steve, for after all, with our modern modes of transportation, he had no reason to ride horses. Overcoming the phobia did not seem necessary, since he is a writer, not a cowboy. During the hypnotic regression, he was taken back to a former lifetime in the early 1800's, when he had been a blacksmith in England. The suggestion was made for Steve to recall his last day as that particular personality. It was then revealed that he had been kicked in the chest by a neighbor's horse—a horse that was normally tame, and one that he had shod many times.

If this was a true regression to a past life of Steve's, it would certainly serve as a means of discovering the traumatic condition that led to Steve Yankee's fear of horses in his current life—a fear he has now overcome.

A friend of mine, whom I'll call Peter and who has since passed away, was an amateur hypnotist who had become extremely proficient at the ancient art. He was of a metaphysical inclination, so it did not surprise me when he told me that he had begun conducting experiments in hypnotic regression to alleged past lives. I thought the process had certain merits, but I frankly informed Peter that he must be on guard against his subjects' unconscious desire to please him by providing him with creative, magnificent—but totally fictional—stories for his tape recorder.

In the following sketches of cases from my late friend's files, we find that whatever psychic-emotional process was involved, its effects on the hypnotized subjects were often cathartic and of extremely practical worth.

One recorded case tells us of a young man who brought his girl friend, Annie K., to see Peter. Annie was so frightened of fire that if someone unexpectedly struck a match or flicked a cigarette lighter anywhere near her, she would often scream. Coupled with her fear of fire was claustrophobia so severe that to be seated in the center of a row of theatre seats would produce nausea and fainting spells. If Annie could not sit on the aisle, she simply could not stay for the film or the performance.

Peter placed Annie into deep hypnosis and moved her through eventful years in her present young life, seeking the cause of the phobic reaction to fire. When none could be found, he suggested that she move back beyond the birth experience of her present life and float through time and space until she could find some occasion when she had been terribly burned.

"Moving back . . . moving back . . . moving back through time, back until you find a time when you were terribly burned. Back to the time which implanted the memory that has made you so frightened of fire within you," Peter's deep voice intones on the recorded tape.

The recording is suddenly shattered by a piercing scream. It continues for nearly a minute until Peter reasserts his control and suggests that the entity that is now Annie move further back to a time less painful. Once this is accomplished, Annie's flat, almost colorless manner of speaking is strangely transformed into a lilting Scottish accent.

The voice claims to be that of Betty, a young actress with a traveling theatrical company in the Scotland of the early 1800's. Peter engages the entity in a dialogue which provides a number of interesting details, and at the same time reveals the young actress as a rather saucy number.

Peter moves her ahead in that life to the time of the fire. The actress's breathing becomes labored, like that of a frightened child being coaxed to sit in a dentist's chair. Peter reassures her, tells her that she may observe everything just as it happened, but that she may view it all dispassionately, as if she were watching a stage performance.

Then, in a most dramatic manner, the actress recounts their performance in a theatre that should have been condemned. Their manager permitted them to go on only after issuing a formal protest to the theatre owner. The worst happened. A heckling drunk in the front row smashed a stage light, and flaming kerosene was thrown against curtains and backdrop. The actors vainly attempted to maintain order and avert panic among the audience; but soon they, too, were swept away by those desperately seeking refuge from the flames. The young actress was trampled by the mob and left to die amidst the fire that rapidly consumed the decaying theatre.

Peter now permits the entity to become further disassociated with the tragedy, at the same time urging it to remember the experience and to place it into proper perspective in its present life. He counts the entity back to the present life as Annie, then permits her to listen to the recorded regression.

Peter's follow-up notes report that Annie's fear of fire left after this one experience. Ordinarily a pyrophobe might be expected to undergo years of analysis, encounter group sessions, psychological therapy, and their attendant financial stresses. Peter seemed to have effected a "cure" in one session of approximately 75 minutes.

Is reincarnation pragmatic? Of course it is. Now let us find out why. Let's stop blaming God for our problems, and let's start facing a reality that may not be easy for all to accept.

# Chapter 2

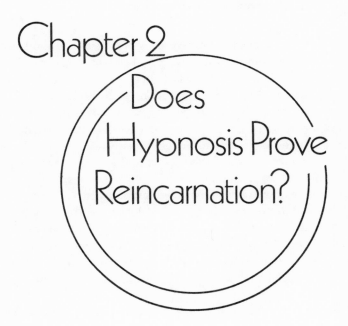

## Does Hypnosis Prove Reincarnation?

Hypnotism is an ancient art, originally practiced by the temple priests of ancient Egypt, Rome, Greece, and Persia. It was not introduced to the modern scientific community, however, until Anton Mesmer, a Viennese physician of the late eighteenth century, expounded on his theories concerning "animal magnetism."

Although Dr. Mesmer found favor in the court of Marie Antoinette and Louis XVI, the French Academy of Science investigated his work in 1778 and accused him of using

mysticism. In spite of an impressive array of evidence support-
ing hypnotic techniques, the Academy discredited his work.
The modern utilization of hypnosis began only a hundred
years ago, and its application to past-life recall is even newer.

Although some people are willing to acknowledge that
many reported "miracles" may very well have been the result of
hypnotic suggestion, wherein the hypnotist was able to reach
the subconscious realms of the subject and stimulate certain
body functions to bring about healing, we are still very
reluctant to lend credence to whatever proofs hypnotic regression may lend to the idea that we have lived before. Regression
to long-hidden traumas of youth and even infancy have served
as the basis for much psychoanalysis. But can we venture to say
with certainty that we can also regress the individual well
beyond his time of birth to other lives he may have lived in ages
past?

The mind is a powerful tool, but it can also be tricky—
especially that part of it known as the subconscious or
unconscious, where supposedly all records of past events are
kept like the storage banks of an intricate electronic computer.
While much evidence has been gained through hypnotic
techniques which regress the individual to what appears to be
consciousness of past lives, we cannot be certain that other
mental and psychic elements are not involved.

Dr. Louis C. McHenry is a professional hypnotist who holds
doctorates in Divinity and Philosophy. He is a member of the
Washington (State) Hypnotists Association, the International
Platform Association, the Northwest Society of Professional
Hypnotists, and several research foundations. He is also
associated with several international yoga groups. Dr. McHenry and his wife operate the Paradox Institute in Kennewick,
Washington, where they teach yoga, hypnotism, and other
metaphysical subjects. Prior to devoting himself to the
metaphysical field, Dr. McHenry was in the world of finance

and banking, but he felt that his life's work must be in helping others find their full potential. He gave up his position as a bank executive in 1970 in order to devote his full efforts to the work of Paradox Institute.

I asked Dr. McHenry for his comments on the infallibility of hypno-regression in proving past lives:

"Frankly, I do not believe hypnotic regression to be infallible. As a child, the subject may have read a story or seen a movie. This story or movie could have depicted something that was close to the circumstances this subject experienced in a past life. He could confuse the two events and bring them together. To a small child, this can happen very easily. He may hear a story or see an event or watch a movie and then put it together and intermingle it with his own experience. It becomes a part of that individual. It would be very difficult to know the difference under hypnosis.

"I will say that there is a high degree of accuracy in regression, but another problem is how to ask questions. I have heard questions in regressions which were put in such a way to the subject that they suggested the answer. This can cause erroneous things to happen. Remember that the subject under hypnosis is in deep rapport with the operator or hypnotist. The hypnotist *may* be desirous of certain answers, and the subject may very well give it to him in the way he wants it, because when in deep hypnosis, the subject is in a very cooperative mood.

"When a person is in a deep hypnotic state, he will have an extreme sense of awareness. His ESP factor is very high. Therefore, if people in the room are not trained to keep their minds blank, they may transmit answers to the hypnotized subject. Then the subject will bring them out, not from his subconscious mind, but from the thoughts of whoever was mentally projecting in the room at that time."

There are many who point to telepathy as a strong

possibility, during hypnosis, and this may be true in many cases. The subject's psychic ability increases during the hypnotic state, and it is not unreasonable to suggest that he might literally pick up the thoughts of others—living and dead. If, indeed, thoughts are able to flow continually through the ether, long after the original thinking has turned to dust, it may be possible for someone at a later time to pick up these thought-forms still permeating the ether.

The hypnotized subject, or the individual in meditation, may be able to pick the mental images out of the ether and relate to someone from the past with whom he is in rapport. This is not as remote a possibility as one might think, and it is certainly no more outlandish than some other existing theories. It has been stated that the first word uttered on this planet is still drifting around somewhere, so who is to say the first silent thought is not also still in the psychic atmosphere which surrounds Earth?

Another prominent theory concerns the idea of possession. While it may not be a pleasant alternative, it is, nonetheless, one we must consider. As Dr. McHenry says: "I have run into this in cases of my own, where the individual does not regress to a former life, but becomes, under hypnosis, a trance medium, and allows another entity to come through and relate his experiences during earth life. This seemingly would indicate that the subject had dropped back into a past life of his own, but actually the discarnate entity was using the subject to come through during the trance state."

The past few years have brought about numerous organ transplants, including hearts and kidneys, taken from one body and placed in another. Cornea transplants are common and quite successful. Reports in recent years tell of Soviet scientists who have removed the head of one dog and placed it on the body of another with apparent success. Brain transplants are allegedly being considered. In the case of possession, we are considering soul transplants!

Brad Steiger writing in *Other Lives* (Hawthorn, 1969) tells of a case that took place in September 1968. A young sergeant named Ed, home from Vietnam and suffering from war injuries, came to hypnotist Loring G. Williams and told him he was being possessed by the spirit of his younger brother Marty, who had died just a short time before.

Williams had never believed in the possibility of possession, although he was open to the theory of reincarnation. The sergeant told how his brother had been killed in a gun accident at age fourteen. He had been very strong physically and was six feet tall when he was thirteen. At the funeral Ed heard a whispered voice promise that Marty would look after him. Sergeant Ed returned to Vietnam where he was involved in a battle, was wounded and blacked out, and was left for dead. At this point the body was allegedly taken over by Marty, who caused the body of Ed to act with superhuman strength, enabling him to get to the hospital and receive needed medical treatment, despite wounds in three places and a great loss of blood. The doctors were amazed that the wounded man was able to make it to the base hospital. Ed was never able to remember anything after the blackout caused by the battle wounds.

The sergeant told Williams that it was apparent to him that the spirit of his younger brother, Marty, had indeed saved his life. It was also obvious that Marty liked the feeling of being in a physical body again. He told of Marty's persistent efforts to take over his body again. The approach of his dead brother was always accompanied by chill, a prickly sensation, and goose pimples on the skin.

Ed was taken by Williams to the home of Professor Charles Hapgood, a man of varied experience in this field, who had dealt with similar cases in the past. Ed was put into a hypnotic trance by Williams, and Marty took advantage of the situation by speaking through his brother's vocal chords. Marty insisted that he only wanted to protect Ed. Professor Hapgood told Marty how much his possession attempts upset his brother. Marty said that he was not aware of this, but that he would continue to possess Ed's body whenever he felt like it.

After the hypnotic session Ed heard the tapes of his brother speaking through him, and told Williams and Professor Hapgood that he felt Marty wanted a test of strength. Marty had always been able to best his brother in any contest of physical strength, but Ed said he now felt that he had the muscle power to win such a contest.

Professor Hapgood related that as soon as he and Williams agreed to such a strange battle, the entity (Marty) immediately took over the body of his brother Ed. Physical features changed to resemble those of a fourteen-year-old boy, with contortion of expression, like that of a frustrated child. The body stood up and attempted to raise a heavy chair by one leg. Marty did not accomplish the feat, but he claimed the contest was unfair, for Ed was trying to push him out of the body. He wanted to try again.

It was agreed that Marty could do so, but first Ed would be given a chance to raise the chair, which he did with little effort. Ed mentioned that in the past, when his younger brother was alive, Marty had been able to best him at this often.

Marty once again inhabited the body of Ed and attempted to raise the chair, but again failed. With grimacing and facial contortions that reminded Williams of Dr. Jekyll and Mr. Hyde, the body, with Marty in control, tried to lift yet another chair, but failed again, even after trying with the other hand. Marty admitted that he had been bested by his brother and agreed to stop possessing Ed's body. He said that he would leave, but should Ed ever need him, he would come back to help him as he had in Vietnam.

I have discussed this idea of possession with various psychics who have discounted the theory, saying in essence that no decent entity would deliberately take over the body of another, causing that in-resident spirit to be set adrift in the midst of an incarnation. True, no *highly developed* spirit would do so. But need we consider only the more spiritually developed entities? What about "demon possession?" Did anyone ever imply that such cases involve a highly developed breed of ethical entities?

The book, and later the motion picture, *The Exorcist,* probably brought the idea of possession home to more people than anything else has for many years. It has also probably been responsible for more cases of pseudo-possession than anything since the epidemics of erotomania and possessism in the Middle Ages.

I do not personally believe possession is as common as some people think, but by the same token, I do not rule it out as a possible alternative to reincarnation. Demon-possession may well have been a part of the cosmology of the churches of the Middle Ages, but it may also be found in certain elements of truth remaining to this day. Could it be that some cases of insanity are actually examples of such demonic forces pushing aside the original entity and taking up residence in the vacated physical body? The Roman Catholic Church, and a few Protestant churches, still retain priests and ministers who are designated as exorcists. Whether they are highly trained psychologists, simply working at the mental level of parishioners who believe they are possessed, or whether they are truly working with entities from another realm who have actually inhabited the body of another may be questioned.

In the case of possession—demonic or otherwise—the physical brain cells would probably continue to operate as before, with current life memories and mannerisms. But certain mental levels and memories common to the new spirit entity would encompass the body, adding new personality traits that were not there before. The personality of this person might change drastically, or show only subtle changes that were detectable only to those closest to him.

In possession, or soul transplant, we would still be dealing with the past life of *some* entity in regression, and whether it was the original entity or another might make little difference, for it would still be an affirmation of reincarnation. In a sense, of course, reincarnation itself is a matter of possession in that the entity enters the physical body, either during the fetus stages or shortly after birth. Possession as we are referring to it here is a changing of entities at some later point in the life of the personality.

It was cold and blustery, the first snowy day of the season, as I got off the "el" from Chicago and walked up the street in Oak Park to the Chicago Psychic Center founded by Clifford Royce, Jr., and now headed by his attractive widow Eursula.

I had met Eursula once before, a short time prior to Clifford's passing, and I knew that as a Spiritualist, Clifford had not put too much stock in the idea of reincarnation. I was not sure of Eursula's thoughts along this line, but in Clifford's final days of this life he presented some thought-provoking ideas that Eursula was still pondering.

"I must admit," Eursula commented, "that I'm still kind of swayed in two different directions, simply because my husband was never a Reincarnationist. Yet the week before he died, he accepted reincarnation, which I felt was quite fascinating.

"Another thing that literally blew my mind was that a week before Cliff went into the hospital, he went into a trance. A spirit guide that has been speaking through him for many years came through, and I asked her many questions about how the spirit actually contacts the body, how they talk through it and whether they take over the whole body.

"She told me that during trance, spirit takes over through the mind itself, through the brain—it controls the brain. They don't come through the whole body. It's like an energy that comes to the brain. They control that part of the brain, and they put part of you to sleep, a deep trance. They control the mechanisms of the eyes, the voice box, everything.

"Then she told me that my husband, who was the mediator, had been her lover in her last life. Now the odd thing about it is that she was a black woman, and my husband has always been attracted to black people. He has always related to black people. She had to ask permission from a higher force, whether she could tell me this or not.

"Why they told me at that point, I can't understand, because we've asked them many questions on reincarnation, and they keep answering, 'We have not seen it'. Yet, when the last moments of the transition were beginning to take place, they told me that there *was* such a thing as reincarnation. You can imagine what this did to me, after all these years of not believing in reincarnation.

"I really believe that Clifford accepted reincarnation as a fact because he was in and out of the body during that last week, and he was trying to relate to me what it was like to be in a coma. He said that it is the experience of going from the light into the darkness, and slowly moving into the light again on another sphere. He said it's really the best way to die—in a coma state. One can relate to this life and to the other life, so that one is in both spheres at the same time.

"I also found out quite recently that Edgar Cayce did not believe in reincarnation until he knew he was going to die. The question is, no matter how much someone knows of death and separation from this life to another, is it fear that makes him want to believe that they will come back again? Is it fear of dying that makes them want to believe that they are living for the fifth or sixth time, that they are an evolved soul, that they know more than anyone else?

"His teacher took him to what he called 'Hell to Heaven on Eight Spheres.' He showed him the different spheres which one would be in in the spirit world, from the lowest to the highest. When he got to the eighth sphere, it was all light, all Being, all God at that particular point. He said that it is a matter of choice, that one would choose whether or not he wanted to come back. The return could be as what we would accept as spirit guides or teachers on a spiritualistic level, or in a physical body to evolve spiritually. So the concept that Clifford gave me in that last week sounded real to me and it really got me thinking.

"I had somebody tell me one time that I had lived in France, and I remember, somewhere back in my mind, that I was holding a baby. I saw bombings, and I died with the baby in my arms. I have a horrible fear of war movies, or anything about war. I have to ask myself the question: Are these memories of my own, or am I picking up the experiences of someone else who actually lived such experiences? Have I taken on someone else's fear? I'm wondering where do I belong, whom do I believe at this point?"

She is prompted perhaps by the fact their eleven-year-old son, Clifford III, is a strong believer that we have indeed trod this earthly soil before, with physical evidence that helps to substantiate the idea.

"In regard to phobias from alleged past lives, I feel that if we did a psychological study of the individual, we could probably very easily see, even to the time that he was in the womb, what it was that he had built that fear around. I have a son who from the time he was able to walk, the time he was able to talk, has had a passion for knives. Dr. Ian Stevenson did some research on him, because he was doing some study on children who seem to remember past lives. Dr. Stevenson came out with the theory that every child who remembered his past life had a scar on his body—some kind of a birthmark—that related to the way he died.

"Well, my son has this type of scar that goes from the top of the neck all the way down to his shoulders. Every doctor I've ever taken him to has asked me how he was stabbed. My son claims he was killed with a knife, or with a sword, by a bunch of renegades. They came to the rice field where he was working with his men, killed his wife and his family!

"I have another son, twelve years of age, who has no birthmarks of any kind. He absolutely does not believe in reincarnation. He pretends not even to know what we're talking about.

"My older son has a deeper knowledge of life, a deeper knowledge of the concept of human beings, but you can take him to a store and ask him to pick out something, and he'll pick out a sword or a knife. I have had to watch him since he was a child, because when he becomes angry the first thing he'll go to is a knife. I used to have to hide all my knives in the house.

"Dealing with spirit activity, spirit guides, spirit teachers as a Spiritualist, I have had the opportunity to talk to spirits. I very definitely have met entities which have been in the spirit world for a long time. I think the oldest one I have met would probably go back 500 years. I have seen death; I have seen the spirit leave the body; I am able to walk into hospital rooms and see the aura leave the body at the exact time of death, and it's like an energy, it's sort of a white smoky substance that becomes greyish. Sometimes it leaves from the top of the head and I've seen it leave from the chest area, sometimes from the nose.

"I feel this is why I question reincarnation. If I'm able to see these spirits and am able to relate to the lifetime of these spirits, then why are they here? Why are they in someone else's body? Why are they living out a Karmic debt?

"There are many theories which we could go into—probably Reincarnationists would have beautiful answers to give you, but the closest thing I've come to is that we are

energy. As the energy begins to evolve, we come back to the
energy that once was, then we evolve more."

There are still other alternatives to the reincarnation theory.
In the story of *The Three Faces of Eve* we see an example of what
might happen should three separate personalities come into
play at various times. This type of condition may represent
either possession or the possibility that three past personalities
that come forward at various times to play their parts, then
vacate to allow another personality to come forward. In a sense,
without the exaggeration and dramatics of the book, this
probably happens to all of us, considering the idea that we are
today the result of what we were in all of our yesterdays. To the
average individual the changes are not as drastic as those
experienced by Eve, who finally was able to meld the three into
one harmonious whole.

Another hypothesis is accepted quite widely, and for that
matter is a theory that I seriously considered during my early
years of research on the idea of rebirth: genetic memory.

Dr. Walter and Mary Jo Uphoff, writing in *New Psychic
Frontiers* (Colin Smythe, Ltd., 1975) commented that there are
several fascinating aspects to hypnosis. "Hypnotic states," write
the Uphoffs, "can take the individual back into memories and
recollections of early life, childhood, infancy, and in some
instances, to purported previous lifetimes." They point out that
one alternative theory is that of "racial memory," the accumulation of the experience of generations, transferred in some way
from one generation to another. Yet another view is Jung's
theory of "collective unconsciousness," in which, under certain
conditions, the individual draws upon the storehouse of
memories and impressions which are a common heritage of the
human race.

Consider for a moment that our genes carry with them the

messages that determine the color of our eyes, hair, and skin. They determine whether we are to be tall or short, stocky or thin, and a multitude of other physical features. Is it beyond reason to think that we might also have the memories of our ancestors locked in our genes?

Where the theory continues to seem logical to me is in the fact that I have certain memories or visions of life in the Middle Ages in Scottish and English castle surroundings. As a youngster I dreamed of castles, knights in armor, and other scenes depicting life in the Middle Ages. Admittedly, I was interested in this period of history, and I read many books based in this era, but in the dreams I seemed to be on the sidelines — an observer seeing royal soldiers and knights in armor riding on horseback, crossing moats in the area of castles. I can visualize life in those large, drafty and damp castles as realistically as I can remember certain events from my early childhood in this life in Richmond, Indiana; Lima, Ohio; or Elmhurst, Illinois.

My grandfather Graham was the family historian and an amateur genealogist. According to his elaborate records, we were direct decendants of Scottish nobility (as well as a few Scottish horse thieves!). My maternal ancestors were also of Scottish lineage, but that side has never been as accurately traced.

The point here is not to romanticize my ancestral past, but to show some just cause for the "memories" of castle life, Scotland, and the British Isles in general. Although I am reasonably convinced that my visions of that era were from a previous life when I was a monk-scribe living in a castle, there is still that strong chance that my genes are providing me with those memories. I have other memories or visions of a lifetime in Rome, and still others of periods in Egypt, thousands of years ago. This, of course, could be genetic memory if you consider the Roman invasions of the British Isles, and the fact that there was a reasonable amount of trade (and intermarriage) between the ancient Romans and Egyptians.

I doubt very much that there are many people living today, with perhaps the exception of natives in remote areas of the world, who do not have the blood lines of several nationalities, considering the invaders, traders, and world travelers who have intermarried or cohabited with the local peoples on their wanderings.

The genetic memory theory certainly would have more appeal to the average person, who is not structured in metaphysical thinking.

That genetic memories of certain ancestors are retained, well within the scope of traceable genealogy, seems to be a logical theory, but it does not answer the complete change of race, mores, and customs from one lifetime to the next when only a few generations separate the two lifetimes.

How does the genetic memory theory explain an individual who recalls a past life, perhaps two hundred years ago, as an African slave being shipped to the Colonies, when the regressed subject is of Danish ancestry. How, in anybody's imagination, can this individual relate a former life, *genetically*, to a member of the black race, when with little research he can trace his immediate ancestry back several generations to Copenhagen?

Whether it is truly past-life recall or one of several alternatives such as ESP, genetic memory, possession, or delusions of memory, we may never fully know, but after many years of study and research in this field, I am willing to give reincarnation a healthy 9 on a scale of 10.

# Chapter 3

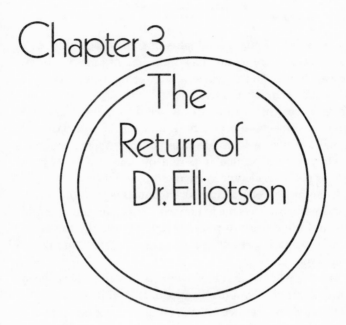

## The Return of Dr. Elliotson

No, we cannot say with absolute certainty that hypnosis—or anything else—*proves* that we have lived before, and that we can reach those earlier times through altered states of consciousness. But if we believe that the subconscious mind is the repository of all memory—even those minute details we are prone to forget only moments after they happen—then who is to say that past-life recall via the dream state, or any other altered state of consciousness, is not accurate? If we are indeed souls with temporary bodies, is it not logical that the memory banks are a part of this individuality or soul of each of us, and that all past lives are retained as three-dimensional movies in which 'we are the "stars," available for viewing when the right combination of circuits is activated?

We do have what appear to be well-documented cases of hypnotized subjects' slipping back into the distant past and bringing forward evidential material that shows a direct connection with a particular period of time that *could* have been their previous lifetime in another physical body.

In listening to Peter's tapes, I encounter again and again men and women who came to him with fears, hangups, mental blocks, and I find them dispelled through what, in some cases, seem to be scenarios, ready-made dramas in which the subject can play a role.

A woman who is afraid of water is found to have been drowned in a pond by a disgruntled husband in another life. Once this incident has been recreated (we cannot discount the fact that it may have been *totally* created) and the subject has heard the recording, her fear of water vanishes.

A middle-aged woman, afraid that her husband is being unfaithful, learns through her reincarnational regression that in a past life she was herself an unfaithful husband, and "her" long-ago wife is her present husband. In this framework, she learns that the Karmic harvest is being reaped. She resolves to be a more loving wife and to make herself more attractive so that her roaming husband will be content at home.

A prim young man with an inordinate distaste for even the slightest bit of uncleanliness finds that he was once a slovenly boor, a glutton and a wine bibber who died choking on his own vomit as he lay in drunken stupor in a pigsty. His revelation is that in this life he must attain a balance between the clean and the unclean.

In each instance, Peter's cases sound like impromptu psychodramas. The men and women who have come to him for regressional therapy begin by stating their problems in the flat, nasal, grumbling, or mumbling speech patterns of their present real lives. Then, under Peter's hypnotic suggestion to regress to a time when their difficulty began, their voices burst out in a variety of accents, reflecting life styles and personal philosophies often in great contrast to their present lives.

Can it be possible that the recall of a crisis situation experienced fully as emotional catharsis can dissolve a long-held phobia?

But isn't that exactly what conventional psychoanalysis seeks to bring about in its years of 50 minute hours? Many practitioners of the healing arts, including medical doctors, osteopathic physicians, chiropractors, and psychic healers, have attributed present conditions of a person's health to matters at submerged levels of consciousness. Recent findings by a large Midwestern medical clinic indicate that psychosomatic conditions may account for as much as 80 percent of all sickness. For many years the medical profession has realized that much sickness is psychosomatic in origin, even though the problem may have become very real by the time medical advice is sought. Through a series of personal dialogues—or patient monologues—the traditional psychoanalyst pries on and on until the patient achieves a breakthrough, remembering the incidents that instituted the trauma that mentally incapacitated him.

What is it that makes us the way we are? As adults, we know that certain events in our childhood play important roles in our present life. If this is the only lifetime we have ever had, then we are certainly heavily influenced by our childhood, but no farther back; we are, as many believe, the products entirely of environment and heredity. To the Reincarnationist, however, there are other explanations: the environment is not limited to this singular life, and heredity may be more spiritual than physical. Psychologists and psychiatrists dwell on the traumatic experiences of childhood as affecting the adult, but they fail to allow for perhaps even greater traumas that took place hundreds or thousands of years ago in the "childhood" of our individuality. If you hate your father, the reason might be found by probing the reaches of the unconscious mind until you find a genuine cause in a past life, rather than simply saying that he caused a trauma in your infancy.

Can a past-life recall show us how to overcome certain fears and phobias or how to benefit from talents we may have possessed in times past? Can chronic illness be traced to a past-life injury and alleviated solely upon receiving this knowledge through recall? Can a tangled web, woven in this life, be traced to its origin in a former existence and unwound satisfactorily? Did Peter really bring these men and women back to other lives? Or did he simply permit their creative psyches to whip up a dramatic structure that could pry their phobias loose from their paralyzing grip?

Again, from a truly pragmatic point of view, *does it really matter?* Whether we regard reincarnation as belief or as a psychic framework, it seems to be a benefactor for countless men and women who struggle against ostensibly inexhaustible demons that make their exterior social lives an endless hell.

While we are dealing with a subjective matter in the principle of reincarnation, we are approaching the topic as fact, not pure speculation. Although scientific testing has neither proved nor disproved the idea, we must admit that reincarnation is at least a logical hypothesis, every bit as valid as the long-established teachings of life after death.

All too obviously, most medical and psychological counselors reject the idea, and choose to remain in the static world of Freudian concepts, which blame all ills on perverted sex drives, parent hate, and the death wish. Perhaps they fear approaching this ancient truth because by so doing they might enable their patients to solve their own problems. Yet since the earliest days of man's recorded history, and perhaps for eons before that, the principle of rebirth has found favor with philosophers, clergymen, and the deep thinkers of antiquity. And today it is finding a practical application in actual medical practices of such men as C. Norman Shealy, M.D.

In February 1975 I had a most interesting interview with Dr. Shealy at the Pain Rehabilitation Center, a unit of St. Francis Hospital in La Crosse, Wisconsin. Dr. Shealy is recognized as one of the most knowledgeable authorities on pain in the United States. He is a neurosurgeon, chief of neurosurgery at Gunderson Clinic, La Crosse, and is associated with the neurology sections of both the University of Wisconsin and the University of Minnesota. He is a graduate of Duke University, and was first exposed to the phenomenon of extrasensory perception and the work of Dr. J.B. Rhine during his undergraduate work at Duke. I asked Dr. Shealy what had prompted his interest in the subject of reincarnation:

"I have believed in reincarnation for a long time, but had very little direct involvement until about September of 1972 hen I was present during a life regression session carried out by Lindsey Jacobs, a psychiatrist from Pittsburgh. I asked Lindsey if he would do a regression on me. He did a regression while I was in a state of reverie, not a deep hypnotic trance. I was able to see myself during a past life. After it was over I wasn't sure, of course, but it was very interesting.

"When the session was completed, I had a period of about two hours of intense clairvoyance. When that was over I went into a very interesting state of mind for several hours. Soon I began to use it occasionally as an aid in gaining insight into patients' problems.

"In February of 1973 I was sitting in a lecture room in Colorado, sorting my slides, as I was the next speaker. Bill Kroger was giving a talk on hypnosis. He was giving the history of hypnosis and mentioned the name John Elliotson.

As he did that I felt a shock go up my spine, and I sat up and said, 'My gosh, that's me!' It was a very peculiar feeling! I knew many of the names he was talking about."

(Dr. John Elliotson was one of the leading physicians in the late eighteenth century—professor of medicine at London University and president of the Royal Medical Society. Dr. Elliotson's work in hypnosis caused considerable interest in the medical profession, and added credibility to the use of hypnotism in the treatment of mental as well as physical disorders.)

"I went up to Bill after his talk was over and I asked him about Elliotson. He told me all he knew about him—that he was a British physician who demonstrated that you could do surgery on patients who were mesmerized. I came home and I asked two medical librarians if they could find something about John Elliotson, but they could not.

"I went to England in June of 1973, and I tried to find out something about Elliotson. One day I was in a cab at lunchtime, on my way to the Royal College of Surgeons. As we came down a street and turned right, I had a very eerie feeling. I looked behind me, and halfway down the block, I saw a little brick Victorian building. I had a very funny feeling about that building—the same kind of feeling I had the day I heard Elliotson's name.

"The next day, I was in that building, which turned out to be where Elliotson had practiced medicine. He was the first professor of medicine at University College, London. I learned a great deal about Elliotson, and it felt very comfortable to me. In fact, when I went into that building I felt a sense of something being wrong, because it had obviously been changed a great deal since Elliotson was there.

"This particular episode, and others, caused me to think I was Elliotson. There are certain similarities in our makeup. I have portraits of him, and while I cannot see a likeness, several friends seem to see physical similarities.*

"Elliotson had a certain distinguishing characteristic— striking black hair. As a child in my current life, I wanted black hair so badly that once, when I was perhaps five or six years of age, I cut a big lock of hair off an aunt who had black hair— and got one of the spankings of my life! When I was sixteen I dyed my hair black, as I still wanted black hair. I realized then that it was ridiculous—too much trouble to dye one's hair black—and I gave it up; but only after I had the experience of dying it black.

"Elliotson was the first physician in London to give up wearing knickers; and you know, when he was in his prime in London, physicians and other proper people wore knickers and white sockst But he refused to do it. He caused quite a stir. As a child, in this life, when I was about nine years of age, I would lie down on the floor and scream and refuse to wear knickers to school, even though all my classmates were wearing knickers. I would wear short pants or long pants, but no knickers!

"Elliotson had a limp, which was apparently a congenital problem. When I was ten years of age had osteomyelitis of my right knee, and was told by the physician that I would always walk with a limp. It really made me angry, so, through determination, I was walking without a limp in six months.

"Now to get on with the really important things about Elliotson. When he was about forty years of age he became quite disenchanted with medicine; he felt that it was boring, that there wasn't much to it. You know, in his day things weren't exactly at an advanced stage. (I'm not sure they are awfully much better today!) At any rate, he learned the

---

* Author's Note: I saw two pictures of Elliotson later that day, and there were some mild similarities between the two men.

techniques of mesmerism from a Frenchman and became quite enchanted with it. He began putting patients into a mesmerized state, and would demonstrate this in public and in the amphitheatre in University Hospital in London. Among his close circle of friends were people like William Thackeray, who wrote a book dedicated to John Elliotson, called *Dr. Goodnough,* and Charles Dickens, whom he taught mesmerism.

"Elliotson demonstrated, for the first time I think, that mesmerized people were capable of doing clairvoyant diagnosis. He often demonstrated this on ward-rounds when he would mesmerize a patient and have that person diagnose another patient whose symptoms were puzzling the physicians. It's rather interesting that one of the things I had wanted to do was to test the ability of clairvoyants to do psychic diagnosis, and just a month *before* I heard the name Elliotson, I had begun a project with a psychic from the Psychic Research Foundation in Chicago.

"Elliotson was quite flamboyant in many respects. He was the youngest person on the faculty of the college, and he had made his reputation by delivering public lectures before he became professor of medicine. He had been promoted by a man named Wakely, who was the first publisher and editor of *Lancet.*

"*Lancet* in those days was a 'rag' — a second-rate tabloid. Yet Wakely, in a rabble-rousing way, promoted Elliotson's work. But when Elliotson became interested in mesmerism, Wakely could not accept this technique, and the two had a falling out. Actually, Wakely had better insight into what it was than Elliotson did, and he considered it all a figment of the imagination. Elliotson insisted that it was a transfer of magnetic fluid, or energy, from one person to another.

"Elliotson introduced narcotics into popular medical use in England. This is rather interesting, since one of my chief goals in my current life is to *keep* people from using drugs and narcotics. I spend a tremendous amount of time trying to talk people out of using narcotics and tranquilizers.

"After two or three years, with a lot of angry editorials and articles written by Wakely, the Board of Trustees asked Elliotson to stop using mesmerism. They told him he was a fine physician, but he had to give up this nonsense. Essentially, one gets the impression from the way it was reported, that Elliotson got very angry and resigned in a huff, which unquestionably is exactly what I would have done. He then took up printing an independent journal, *Der Zeist*, which he published for about twelve years; but it was never too successful. Also, before he resigned as professor of medicine at University Hospital, he demonstrated the use of mesmerism in surgery, just as Mesmer had done. Elliotson was the first to do it in the English-speaking world.

"Elliotson died a somewhat bitter old man, because he was totally rejected after he resigned from the university, and he was never really prominent after that. He essentially lost his place in medical history in England because of this. Certainly many other contributions were made by Elliotson, including the introduction of the stethoscope in England. These would have made him very significant in medical history if it were not for his taking up with this parapsychology.

"After I began to feel very comfortable about this whole business I learned more about Elliotson, and felt very strongly that this had been me.

"I think one could look at it in one of two ways: Either I was John Elliotson and am John Elliotson reincarnated; or somehow—clairvoyantly, precognitively, or in some other way—I knew there was a message in John Elliotson's life that I should read. In either case, it seems to me there was certainly parapsychological extrasensory perception involved in my reaction to Elliotson's name and the other life."

I asked Dr. Shealy if his personal knowledge of past lives had helped shape his present goals, and he commented: "Interestingly, all of this has led me to a feeling that my reason for being here, at the current time, is to teach my fellow physicians something about holistic medicine. We have put too much energy into the mechanistic approach to medicine and not enough into the psychological approach.

"You see, I was in perhaps the most mechanistic of all specialties, neurosurgery. I have evolved pretty far away from that, and I am getting a Ph.D. in psychology at the moment from the Humanistic Institute. I feel that my purpose is to point this out to people, and a psychic some time ago confirmed this. Although I didn't tell him of my presentiments, he said that this was my purpose in this life, and that if I did not achieve this goal, I would come back as a politician!

"Elliotson, as I look at it, muffed his opportunity to invent psychology, to develop the whole field of psychology and psychiatry. He did not understand the tremendous importance of mesmerism in terms of the psychological techniques. Of course there was no psychology or psychiatry at that time.

"About five or six years ago a medical writer, Arthur Freese, came here and did a paper for *Popular Mechanics* about my work. When I first met him, I had a real problem relating to him; I felt rather hostile toward him, but controlled it. When I received the proofs of the article, I just flipped—it was horrible! He claimed, and I believe him, that it had been totally rewritten by the editor. However, when the paper finally came out, it was quite good. He then came back a couple of times and did several other articles on my work. Later he did an article that appeared in *Parade* magazine, which gave the Pain Center the kind of public attention it needed to become really established here.

"Interestingly, just prior to my learning about Elliotson's life, Art had wanted to do a biography of me. I told him that I thought that would be an utter waste of time, that he couldn't possibly sell a biography of me. But I suddenly decided on the spot to ask him to write a book on parapsychology with me. I spent about three hours telling him about my work with the psychics. He got very excited about it, and we agreed to write a book together. I'm quite convinced that Art was Wakely and that our writing this book together was a resolving of our Karmic relationship, which was antagonistic over parapsychology in the last life. I gave him remarkable freedom in writing the book; I wanted to write it, but I allowed him to do so in his style. I told the story because I felt it was important that I not fight with him over it. Good or bad, we shall see. There is no question, I would have written the book quite differently [*Occult Medicine Can Save Your Life*, Dray Press, 1975].

"I have asked more than twenty psychics throughout the country about this, and interestingly every one of them has said, 'Yes, you were John Elliotson.' Another coincidence is that I had a peculiar feeling about Mesmer before I knew about Elliotson. I had had a very strong attraction to Mesmer's life, and it even vaguely made me wonder whether I could have been Mesmer, or somehow been associated with him.

"Henry Rucker, a psychic healer with whom I work, told me before I knew about Elliotson that he thought I had been involved in mesmerism but that I had not been Mesmer himself. I have had, since then, a couple life regressions done on me in which I have looked at various aspects of Elliotson's life, but I don't think you could consider them legitimate experiences, since I knew so much about him by then.

"Reincarnation and karma are very hard to prove, but I feel very comfortable with it. After these various things that have happened, I psychically feel reincarnation is a fact."

The insights of Drs. Shealy/Elliotson are most enlightening, for here is a modern medical doctor, with credentials that would take a full page to list, talking of the practical application of an ancient concept that until recently has been locked in musty editions of metaphysical volumes. Dr. Shealy has thoroughly researched the field of hypnotic regression and believes that regression can ferret out certain deep-seated problems which cannot be probed through conventional Freudian methods— nor those of Adler or Jung, for that matter: It is unfortunate that more psychiatrists have not used regression as a technique for getting at problems in patients, à la Kelsey in *Many Lifetimes* (Doubleday 1967). Denys Kelsey said to me, "In a maximum of twelve hours of regression therapy I can accomplish what will take a psychoanalyst three years!"

I asked Dr. Shealy how he uses knowledge of reincarnation in his counseling:

"A while back there was a male patient at this hospital who was attracted to a woman patient. They had an affair going, and this was a bad situation. He was married, although she was single at the time.

"I was able to give him a past-life reading in which I saw him married to his present wife in three past lives. This seemed to make him realize that there was a strong emotional tie between them, and he broke off the affair with the other woman. That, of course, is just one small example of how regression can be used in counseling."

While the Freudian school of psychoanalysis depends heavily on perverted sex drives, parental hatred, and the death wish as the bases for most human misery, the analyst who uses the reincarnation principle as his guide suspects that our problems may date back much farther than childhood. He acknowledges that our loves, hates, and environments are not the end result of what we are today, but are probably in themselves the effect of causes created long before birth into this present life.

Once a basic knowledge of past lives is known, the trained analyst, whether a psychic counselor, psychologist, or medical practitioner, can put the pieces together, like a picture puzzle that will show the "why" and "what" of the problem, and often the "who" as well. As you will read later, such therapeutic application of past-life awareness is being used to great advantage in the counseling of psychiatrists and other medical doctors, psychologists, and psychic healers.

# Chapter 4

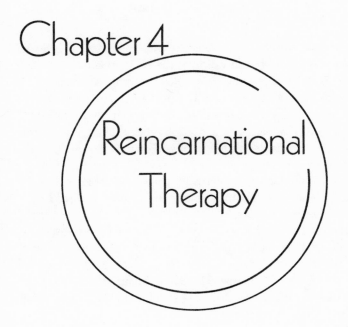

# Reincarnational Therapy

Robert R. Leichtman, M.D., of Sausalito, California, is a physician who has practiced internal medicine and psycho-somatic medicine for many years. During this time he has been repeatedly impressed with the profound influences individual mental and emotional factors have on the course of illness and on the physical, psychological, and material well being of people.

Since 1970 Dr. Leichtman has devoted his time exclusively to the deeper aspects of psychology in order to comprehend them and to use them to modify consciousness and behavior.

Dr. Leichtman was not satisfied with inferences based on indirect testing and observation of the *effects* of consciousness, and he decided that exploration of the psychic dimensions of the human mind by his own ESP would be the only way to get satisfactory and direct answers. "It is apparent to me that consciousness is basically a non-physical quality that is reflected only in observable behavior and mediated only through the physical nervous system and body," Dr. Leichtman says. "The only satisfactory tool that I have been able to use to explore these inner mental dimensions is to do it directly by the so-called psychic means."

Most of Dr. Leichtman's investigative work emphasizes a psychic analysis of current character traits and tendencies. He then adds details of past lives as a means of complementing the analysis of current characteristics, problems, strengths, and potentials, as well as weaknesses—a pragmatic approach to the subject.

"The technique that I employ is a rather simple one," states Dr. Leichtman. Most of his work is referred to him by colleagues or through word of mouth. "The only information that I usually receive is a name, age, and approximate location," he says. "If it is a clinical report that is requested by one of my colleagues, I may get a sentence or two describing a problem in very general terms. I stress that, lest some imagine that I have great volumes of past history and the opportunity for close personal observation to give my imagination clues about their character and past lives."

His colleagues and his individual clients report that the analysis seems to fit their estimation of their character quite well. In his work with health professionals, there is also additional confirmation of accuracy based on their professional observations as well as psychological tests. "I rarely see the cases that I investigate, but I have been fortunate to receive follow-ups and occasionally visit many of these cases." Though confirmation of details of past-life events has been rare, a few subjects have confirmed the stories while under deep hypnosis; however, this is a phenomenon of doubtful value according to Dr. Leichtman.

"The best proof comes in an intangible, but nevertheless strong, intuitive knowing on the part of the subject that the substance of the report *is* correct. It just seems to 'feel right' and 'makes sense' to them. That will seem unscientific, but it probably is the best guide concerning the correctness of the report."

Following are a few illustrative case histories from Dr. Leichtman. By inference, some of the dynamics and laws that seem to govern reincarnation and human relations can be seen.

"One instance in which there is some degree of confirmation of past-life details concerns a lady in her sixties who asked me to check into her immediate past life. Not knowing much about her except her general physical appearance, I launched into a brief summary of her past life in the first five minutes of having met her.

"The important aspects of this life was that she was previously a man who was a rather insensitive and hard-headed person, who managed to involve himself in a group which partly massacred a small settlement in a rather primitive frontier era. As the purpose was to render this settlement powerless, it was largely the men and the adult women who resisted vigorously and were killed. The net result was that many children were left without parents, and many of the mothers were left widowed.

"This person then confirmed the story and added a few details of her own. It seemed that she had had a vivid dream about four years previously, and it contained this episode of the massacre. At first, her reaction had been one of shock and resentment. But then, she related, it seemed to stay with her as being too 'real' to reject out of hand.

"Another reason for accepting such a horrible past was that it seemed to explain a good deal about her current life. She had been raised in an orphanage until her late teens, never having known her natural parents or a normal childhood. Then she was married early to a man who was less than an ideal partner. Shortly after the birth of her sixth child her husband passed on swiftly of natural causes, leaving her a widow with six young children.

"By the time the dream came to her she was a grandmother living alone. Her family was grown, and her main work of this incarnation was finished. There was still resentment and self-pity for all the hardships she had undergone, so the dream was timely for her, as it gave her an insight into herself and told her why her life was as it was."

Dr. Leichtman concluded this case by stating that the patient had found life very difficult, but that she realized she must bear any sacrifice to keep the family together, which she did, in spite of the fact that several of the children developed behavior problems. The practical value is shown in the fact that she was forced to accept the responsibility she shunned in an earlier life, and to atone for the hardships she had created.

"Another interesting problem was a young man who consulted me about his past lives. He was in his late twenties and worked as an accountant for a large business. A few years earlier, he had been horribly injured in an accident and abandoned by the party who was at fault. The injuries were to require hositalization for months and leave him with permanent weakness in his legs and total impotence. He had a rather withdrawn and hostile disposition."

"Important events in this young man's past lives demonstrated the patterns of destiny which related to his illness. In the eighteenth century," Dr. Leichtman says, "the patient had been a soldier from Europe sent to Latin America to subdue the newly conquered territories. He was responsible later for destroying a village and killing a large number of natives, some of whom were mutilated before being killed. His general attitude during that life was a self-righteous contempt for most of humanity.

"In the nineteenth century there was a brief life as a woman who suffered from multiple physical illnesses, ending in a degeneration of the spinal cord and a slowly developing paralysis of her arms and legs. That life was dull and filled with misery and disappointment.

"The entity of the young man was reborn again about the time of World War I in Germany. His parents were poor and discontented with life, as they had to work so hard to survive. His father was hostile and withdrawn.

"When Hitler came to power, this personality recognized in him a new hope for success for himself and his nation. He became caught up in the Nazi movement and ended up denouncing his own father after he tried to restrain him. Later he joined the army and became a zealot in the Nazi cause. After the war began the people of conquered countries did not receive humane treatment from him; one of his major abuses was in raping the women. Still later, he was wounded and abandoned by his comrades, who had to move on in great haste. The enemy was about to capture him and presumably mistreat him when, realizing how desperate the situation was, he shot himself.

"Again, it appears that the harm committed is later visited on the one who inflicts it. His contempt and callous behavior was returned in the form of humiliating and devastating injuries or illness. And the activity of rape returned to haunt him as permanent impotence following injury to his spinal cord."

It was notable in this case, as Dr. Leichtman pointed out, that this was a person with a rather angry disposition, tending to be paranoid, uncooperative, and expressing contempt for human rights. Compassion, tolerance, forgiveness, and a significant capacity for affection were all very minimal. The absence of these strengths seems to have been directly related to how well life treated him.

"Hopefully, this would be a subject in whom insight could bring about a great change. If he were to realize a greater sense of responsibility for his current state and recognize that he must change his attitude toward his humane obligations and people in general, then he could take a major step toward healing his ancient problem. As it was, he had much to be bitter about from the events in this incarnation. His bitterness seems once again to be stronger than his compassion and capacity to forgive. The factual knowledge of these events apparently has not resulted in much change in his disposition as yet."

Dr. Leichtman tells of another lady in her late twenties who requested a life reading for general interest. After it was given, she reported that she was rather aggressive for a woman. In many ways she didn't like being a woman and occasionally wished that she had been born a man. Something of a woman's liberationist, she also reported an unusual fear of knives.

"Significant in her previous lives was the fact that in several male incarnations there was usually a rather aggressive personality which had all the earmarks of male chauvinism," Dr. Leichtman learned. "This was quite marked in several recent lives.

"In her most recent life, she had passed on after something she had dreaded strongly for quite a while—cancer surgery. She had a premonition that she was doomed, and it was correct."

Dr. Leichtman offers this as another case in which a fear that once had a realistic basis was carried forward into a new incarnation as an irrational fear.

"The general character trait of being aggressive and a bit self-centered is one that is quite slow to change, persisting for the new incarnation, despite a change of sex. This hints at the concept that male chauvinism and female chauvinism flow from the same reservoir!"

Another case Dr. Leichtman relates is that of a middle-aged

lady executive of a nursing home. About a year previous she had to have her right hand amputated because of cancer. Following the surgery, she had persistent pain in the area of the stump and the not uncommmon phenomenon of a sensation of pain in the now-missing right hand. A psychic analysis on her had been requested by her physician, who was attempting to help her with this rather serious psychological and physical problem.

Dr. Leichtman found that she had been a man rather frequently in past lives during the last few centuries. Often she had been a soldier. During one particular lifetime, at the time of the Crusades, "he" had rather thoroughly enjoyed combat and killing the "heathen." It so happened that his enthusiasm for punishing the heathen was so great that he participated in some torturing of them, as well as some mutilations and other atrocities.

"I found that her present temperament was considerably hostile and aggressive. This was a powerful person who had always expected to be in command of her surroundings and her lifestyle. Subconsciously she was still raging about the indignity of having to endure a mutilating (but necessary) amputation.

"The basic problem was one of continuing and unremitting *lack* of compassion, tolerance, sensitivity for the welfare of others, willingness to cooperate with others, and forgiveness. There was a strong pattern of intolerance and anti-authoritarian tendencies in her. This was coupled with an aggressive urge to dominate people and to cultivate power as a standard of success. There was also a strong inclination to be fault-finding of others and insensitive to the weaknesses and failures of others."

"All these deficiencies along with a recurring tendency to megalomania made her karmically heir to this very unpleasant health problem," Dr. Leichtman analyzed: "It is interesting to note," he pointed out, "that she was attracted to work in a nursing home *before* the amputation. Perhaps it was an unconscious attempt to familiarize herself with the magnitude of suffering from serious physical afflictions even before her own personal tragedy, or it may have reflected a redeeming quality to help balance the scales from the previous life of inflicting torture on others.

"It is also a situation in which one might infer that the physical cancer was preceded by a figurative cancer of her emotions in terms of a malignant aggressiveness and hostility unopposed by compassion or tolerance," he added.

"So now she was saddled with an impossible situation of persistent physical pain without apparent cause and the finality of having to live the rest of her life without her right hand. Surely it was a test of endurance and a situation designed to cultivate tolerance and sensitivity to suffering in even the most stoic.

"One also glimpses the presence of an Overmind, which oversees the coordination of what often appears to by dynamic confusion on the level of the physical plane.

"This story also indicates the type of sacrifice that the immortal essence is willing to take on in order to balance out experiences. It also demonstrates the method that is used to achieve the right lesson—the actual experience of enduring a hardship similar to one inflicted on others earlier. In other words, to develop humane sensitivity to the wrongness of certain acts, those harmful acts are eventually visited on the one who has done harm.

"Implied in the whole episode is the notion that there is some sort of Intelligence that does seek to rectify mistakes and to establish justice. The coordination with exquisitely specific circumstances more than hints at an Intelligence that tran-scends the immortal essence of any one human being."

This record would be incomplete without at least one case of Dr. Leichtman's in which the positive side of life and the evolution of consciousness were given some detail. Where life has been lived nobly and responsibly there is a steady accumulation of talent, wisdom, and compassion that adds grace and beauty to successive incarnations.

"One such person is a middle-aged lady who now lives the life of a housewife with a good family and comfortable means. Her personality bears a certain dignity, yet she is cheerful and outgoing. Her experiences in this life have not all been easy, but she has been able to cope with them with considerable strength and serenity. She has a very good mind which she feeds with careful observations, good books, and intelligent conversation.

"Her past record is filled with positive accomplishments. She held several important posts in the Atlantean era, including religious, healing, and philosophical lifetimes. In the period of ancient Egypt she had several lives devoted to work in the temples of that day. In this way she developed considerable expertise in occult skills and psychic abilities, as well as a deeper appreciation of the invisible forces which guide our destiny.

"In more recent lives she often had to endure far less glamorous lives, which were filled with heavy obligations and challenges. But in each of them she managed to apply her strengths of wisdom and compassion to do her best. As a result, there was a growth of character in even rather mundane circumstances.

"In a quite recent life she had been the Mother Superior of a large convent, and she managed to accomplish a great deal for herself and her charges.

"The record is an honorable one, and it reflects itself in her character today. Partly because of the reading, she had again developed a greater appreciation of her [Catholic] religion and has taken up a more mature study of occult skills and esoteric philosophies. As might be suspected, much insight into her life was already present, but the reading quickened it and stimulated thought along new lines of reflection. On a more mundane level, it explained certain dream symbols and meditative experiences. Her interest in astrology and palmistry was stimulated, and her faith in her own intuitive impressions on these endeavors was bolstered."

This was a case in which the main benefit of the reading was not a matter of having problems explained, but rather of potential assets being revealed and origins given detail. It was perhaps more meaningful for her to have this, as she had a great capacity to comprehend and appreciate these details.

Dr. Leichtman says, "Properly understood, reincarnation is not the curse that some people declare. Nor is it unreasonable and unfair. It is simply the sensible working out of the evolution of consciousness and the development of mature character. One physical lifetime is just not enough, nor would it properly honor the indwelling Spirit."

Along this same path, a recent article in *Psychic Times* contained an interview with a Dr. Gierak, a biologist and chiropractor from California who is also an adept hypnotist. Dr. Gierak uses past-life regression in the treatment of certain conditions, including those he feels have their roots in a past-life trauma.

Dr. Gierak believes that everyone is actually *two people*. One is the physical, which we see, and the other the ethereal (soul). This is a basic metaphysical concept, but Dr. Gierak goes a step further, stating that the ethereal is able to step aside and view the physical objectively. He believes the ethereal can view past lives as an observer, giving the individual a deeper level of self-awareness. At this point the individual is able to turn off pain at the problem area.

"We've already had this interview," Nancy French told

reporter Lois Wille of the *Chicago Daily News* as they sat down for coffee. "You dreamed it Tuesday night."

Reporter Wille confirmed that on Tuesday night she had indeed dreamed of a talk with Nancy French, but that the dream was vague and she could not fully recall what was said. Mrs. French agreed to "review" the interview for the journalist.

Nancy French is a deeply spiritual woman, quite active in her home town Methodist Church in Bettendorf, Iowa. She is the wife of Bill French and the mother of two sons and a daughter. Her work involves teaching courses in Human Love, Spiritual Love, and Parapsychology at Scott County Community College.

We asked Nancy for her thoughts on the practical aspects of reincarnation:

"There is a desperate need for more in-depth counseling. The immediate life—body, personality—is in *such* great need. What I do is not a headline-grabber, but there has to be someone who rolls back the curtain!

"I have known since infancy that survival for the planet absolutely lay in being able to raise the level of awareness. In early childhood this was transferred to me psychically in the form of a recurring dream of a blanket that needed ticking. The blanket, almost on to infinity—was without ticking! *A lot of work to be done!*

"My goal, of course, is to help people see that there is more than just a body, or a mind, or a personality to be dealt with. A dramatic situation occurred during a counseling session with a woman in her late twenties. She was tall, statuesque, and sturdy. She had built a strong body in this lifetime because she wanted to move firmly and with great intent out of a German concentration camp in her previous lifetime in which there was starvation and frailty. I discerned psychically that she wanted to work out some of the fear, anger, and resentment she felt toward the Jewish-German World War II situation. She described her 'memory' of standing at a wire fence as a female child, looking out, only to turn around to see her mother and brother, among others, being taken alive from a truck. Immediately here 'memory' skipped to seeing those two loved ones being incinerated. We were together in the room—the door and window were closed, there were no drafts, but there was an odor of burned flesh! I asked, 'Do you smell the odor?' She, too, was aware of it. As she concluded her story, the odor became fainter. When she left, it was gone. By venting her anger, she'd ventilated those particles that had entrapped her. With forgiveness—and relief—she was able to move out of the scene.

"In this lifetime possibly that woman would absolutely not live anyplace where there was a fence, particularly the chain-link kind. Perhaps she'd feel a subconscious fear whenever she saw an ad for fencing or would avoid any kind of jewelry that appeared as a chain-link design.

"Another woman confided, 'Every time I think of anyone touching the small of my back—and I've even whirled around to hit one of my children—I think someone stabbed me in the back.' I said, "Look at this another way. Who did *you* stab in the back?" Her eyes widened and she realized, 'That's it!' She had received the impact of energy against her body of something she'd done in another lifetime to another person. When she expressed interest in being helped from this practical reincarnation situation, I made a healing in the small of her back with my hand, and she felt much better, lighter. It freed the attention units that had been concentrated on that part of her body."

Ann Fisher is a professional psychic consultant and medium who has an office in Albany, New York.

"I have been told, and have picked up through my own consciousness and through hypnotic age regression, that I have been a psychic in several lifetimes. I was not psychic as a child, but became aware of my psychic ability in 1965 at the age of 23. I was sitting in the audience of a Spiritualist church, seeking a message. The medium asked me to come forward and told me I had this ability in a previous life. This encouraged me to develop my psychic ability, and within three or four months I was able to do readings as well as the medium who discovered me."

Ann holds a degree in psychology from Hartwick College and is known nationally for her outstanding work, in which her clients give her an accuracy rating of 90 percent. She has taught subjects in parapsychology at various colleges, and has traveled nationally lecturing on various subjects in the psychic field. Her specialty is psychometry, although she is well versed in all aspects of metaphysical pursuit. In addition to having her own TV show, "Tuning In With Ann Fisher," she has appeared as a guest on various radio and TV programs throughout the country.

While visiting with Ann in Saratoga Springs, New York, I asked her if she would care to share some cases for this book:

"Anthony L. from Amsterdam, New York, was a thirteen-year-old boy who had a bright yellow aura: He was a very intelligent boy—yet, when he took an IQ test he would score 74, which is borderline moron. The father had given up. He had tried everything, but the boy was not responding.

"He brought Anthony in for a reading and consultation, thinking maybe I could get through to him. The boy normally did not respond well to people, but we established a rapport immediately, and I said to Anthony: 'I know why you're rebelling against authority. You feel you are grown up, and you don't want to be a child. You came back too fast. In your last incarnation you were a very important man in northern Germany. You had a lot of money and prestige, as well as a lot of authority. You somehow put yourself in this lifetime to learn a lesson, to learn to get along with people, but you are not doing very well because you are rebelling against your father, your mother, your teachers, doctors, and everyone you know. My boy, you must remember you are still a child. When you grow up, in a few more years, you can give orders as you did before, but right now you have to live in the world of people as a thirteen-year-old boy.'

"I had three sessions with this boy, and he admitted this is how he felt; even though he was as young as he was, it seemed that I did help him realize that he belonged with other children. I sent him back, asking him to try, and I have heard from his father that he is improving and realizes why he acted the way he did. I believe when they give him another IQ test he will come up with a high score, because he is above normal in intelligence. He was just being miserable, not wanting to show a high score when tested.

"I have found in my own case that in past lives I was a psychic, and in one lifetime I was hanged in England as a witch. My name was Ann then, too. In another life, in Salem, Massachusetts, my name was Sarah B. The year was 1687. I was 35, unmarried, and considered very strange by the townspeople. I would go through a forest and pick some kind of leaf from which I would make a tea. The townspeople accused me of witchcraft. I was tried in 1687, then burned at the stake.

"I can remember being terrified of fire as a child, and my mother and father could never understand why. They thought maybe some other child had scared me. If we were visiting people, I would always stand near a window so I could get out, because I had this fear of being burned alive. We never had a house fire, and I was never in a fire, so I definitely feel this fear goes back to another life.

"I did not flash in with psychic ability in this life until I was an adult. It was 1965, the year that psychic abilities and awareness started to come out in many people and to become acceptable. I had finally been born into an age where I could talk about it, where I could appear nationally on TV and radio, and not be burned at the stake.

"I am now in an age where I can use my psychic ability throughout all my lifetime helping humanity, promoting my case for survival after death. I feel that with my counseling, my being able to tune in on the past, my clients are able to see why they are as they are in this lifetime and possibly why they have certain problems or situations in their present lives. I feel that in many ways they are able to solve their problems because they understand their past.

"As I tell of case histories through my counseling, I feel that I will be able to present some proof that reincarnation does happen and is a real thing. I feel more and more people will come to believe that as we look back in past-life regressions, we are able to understand why we are as we are today."

"Specifically, I would suggest several implications of reincarnation. My experience in obtaining past-life material and my insights into specific individuals and their circumstances lead me to many of these conclusions:

1. "A physical life is just a chapter in a larger volume of 'stories.' Its meaning lies in the basic 'plot' which connects all of the stories in the volume.

2. "The physical personality has its roots in the distant past of previous existences. Degrees of proficiency or maturity, as well as talents and wisdom, have their origins in the entire accumulation of past experiences, rather than just this lifetime.

3. "The state of the accumulated character traits has much to do with the determination of birth conditions. It seems one has to earn the right to favorable circumstances and opportunities in the selection of parents and socio-economic conditions.

4. "The immortal essence is impelled by its own wisdom

and purpose and by Universal Law to see that errors are corrected and compensation is made for earlier indiscretions so that character is perfected.

5. "Understanding the meaning of one's character traits and outer circumstance as being inherited from past activities can lend great insight into the correct perspective about them and an understanding of how to best cope with them.

6. "A glimpse of one's inner purpose gives the reassurance that one is not so much a victim of blind and cruel fate as that one is actually impelled by an inner need to experience what is necessary to express more fully an inner potential. This knowledge leads to a less desperate and more impersonal attitude toward adversity and success in one's life.

7. "A comprehension of the principles of reincarnation will help to take attention off of the outer forms of one's situation in life and focus intelligent attention on conditions in the personality which are the ultimate causes for having attracted those conditions in general.

8. "There is a stimulation of a more humanistic attitude and group consciousness about humanity. We are literally all part of mankind, and we are obliged to consider everyone, within reason, as brothers and sisters.

9. "Life and its events are relevant to the personality's perspectives. There is a Greater Intelligence overseeing conditions and a Universal Law that guides right human relationships. Justice comes eventually. There is a continuity of reward and discipline from one life to the next. Nothing is misplaced or forgotten. Neither the immortal essence nor life is mocked.

"One could speculate much more about reincarnation. Life is mysterious, but probably not blind or purposeless. Reincarnation helps to explain much about these mysteries."

# Chapter 5

## A Father Twice Over

My search for psychic counselors who use the principle of rebirth in their work, at one point led me to Los Angeles, where I met Alice Lane, with whom I had corresponded over the years. Alice is director of The Way of Light at Orcas Island, Washington, and publisher of a monthly magazine by the same name. A psychic astrologer, she frequently uses reincarnation as a basis for finding the origin of her clients' problems.

Psychoanalysts often say that our problems are associated with a hatred for one parent or another, but seldom determine what actually caused that extremely strong emotion. Regression to a former lifetime can often produce just such information, as Alice shows here:

"Only a few years ago I was guided to completely unlearn all I knew about astrology. The higher truth was telling me that if I tuned in totally on the other person's higher consciousness while giving a reading, many truths would be revealed. Since that time I have noted greater accuracy, and what is even more important, recently I have been pleasantly surprised to find that I seem to be on a straight path of communication with the soul of another during the reading. Through the thoughts and revelations shown to me concerning their past and present, I am able to trigger the idea which encourages the inspiration which provides the necessary flow of energy that ties together everything pertaining to the idea.

"My readings are soul readings inasmuch as the astrology map is the only tool on the earth plane to be used in searching for answers to the puzzle of earthly conditions concerning the individual. The natal chart is the blueprint of the subconscious (soul).

"The past is being revealed in various forms through the subconscious energies within each individual memory bank. All the existences one has lived, in which he was not able to cope with the responsibility of truth, and all that he has done unto another are recorded within. As we have done unto others in the past, so be it done unto us in the present, and on and on and on, until higher awareness of truth takes over and one begins to realize the *why's* of it all.

"The very center of one's subconscious is pure spirit, and therefore, when this ray of electricity comes through one's beingness, it registers on the eardrums and in the sensitive parts of one's glands, which in turn registers within the soul and allows the energy release to take effect. Hence, the individual suddenly finds himself in another dimension of time and space, reliving, once again, a traumatic experience, the responsibility of which he was not able to accept in that previous dimension of time and space.

"The following is one example of a flashback to another dimension of time and space, which was necessary for the release of suppressed energy in a past existence:

"A loud, shrill, agonizing scream pierced the large, four-bedroom house, isolated on two and a half acres of land. 'He shot me!' the hysterical outburst continued, 'I couldn't believe it! My own father shot me!'

"Lyn, a client, had suddenly flashed back to a fragment of her soul incarnated in another dimension, as she recalled the catastrophic events taking place.

"All during this lifetime Lyn had felt strongly competitive with her father over her mother. It was awakened within her as a small child of six when the father and mother went away for a few days together, leaving her with her grandmother. The man with whom she was in competition had taken her mother away for a weekend, giving Lyn the feeling that she was being rejected by her mother. She had thought her mother loved her more, but now her mother had deceived her and made a fool of Lyn. Lyn changed in her feelings toward her mother after that incident.

"Consequently, all during Lynn's life, up to now, she had been afraid to form any emotional relationships. Others constantly were deceiving her, and, once betrayed, she never allowed the individual to have another chance."

"The one thing I hate above all," Lyn told Alice Lane, "is hypocrisy. I resent it in any way. I don't like to be made a fool of!" Flashing back in memory to the time as a child, Lyn recalled, "I did really well while they were gone. My grandmother said I did. I tried not to show how I really felt." As the tears began streaming down Lyn's face, she sobbed, "I thought I was in the way! And my father wasn't going to get a chance to laugh at me, because I wasn't going to let him know that it bothered me!"

"Did your father used to laugh at you?" Alice asked.

"No, it was subtle, and even now I just don't know how to work it out. I feel guilty about it, I think, because I've confronted him with it." A new burst of emotional energy released.

"It's coming up now, Lyn, that's okay," Alice told her. "Release all the suppressed energy, and you will feel a lot better once it is gone."

"I think my mother was concerned about me," Lyn spoke up.

"How did you feel about your father?"

"I'm mad at him! He's not doing as he's supposed to be doing," Lyn sobbed.

"What is he supposed to be doing?"

"He's going to want to hear the tape, and I don't . . . ."

"This is a tape of your soul energies," Alice explained. "You don't have to share it with anyone unless you feel guided to do so."

"I think he's . . . he's just flitting his life away! That's a terrible thing to . . . ." Lyn burst into an emotional wave of tears. "And it's his decision to do so. He spends a lot of time reading, and I think he should be working hard at something, not running after rainbows!"

As the interview continued, Lyn recalled many past incidents in this current life involving competition with her father. Suddenly without warning, she flashed back to the past life more significant than any other concerning the competition with her father over the mother.

This was a life in Scotland. Lyn was a young boy of fourteen or fifteen. At that time Lyn and her father (who is again her father in current life) were hunting in the marshland. As she described the cold chilling water of the marsh, a loud scream pierced the air. Lyn was reliving the past life in which her father killed her.

The shock of being shot by her father and left to die was more than she was able to bear. As she lay dying in the icy cold marsh, the father returned once again to finish the job, this time shooting her in the sinus region of the head. Consequently, Lyn has terrible sinus headaches this lifetime.

Upon completion of Lyn's interview, she not only had compassion for her father but totally forgave him for all occurrences of that lifetime.

"Within a few weeks, Lyn began to clean out her closet, throwing away dresses for which she had had a fondness in the past. No longer did they have any attraction for her. Her personality changed to a more positive, friendly, optimistic outlook on life. In the past, Lyn had run away from emotional involvements. Now, she was seeking new ones. This shy, timid girl of the past had begun to blossom into a full-blown beauty with confidence, poise, and openness," Alice reported.

Lyn had been a social worker for the state the past few years and she had counseled many others with their problems. Now, with her added image, she had a better understanding of others and how to work with them.

"Everyone who knows Lyn marvels over the changed personality. As Lyn says, 'I am more of a person than I have ever been in this life.' It is also interesting to note that Lyn has never had a reoccurrence of her terrible sinus headaches. She was so satisfied with the therapy she received during that reading, that she is now a student in one of my classes of astrology, learning the psychic approach."

Alice further says:

"Today many are experiencing soul energies being released from the subconscious.

As a psychic astrologer (intuitive psychologist), I have become more aware of a turning point in my readings and consultations. It appears as if suddenly many hidden remnants of the past are surfacing within the consciousness. As these energies come up to be dissolved, many will flash back to past lives, so they, too, will be freed of bondage to that particular life of pain. Many who have died violent deaths in the past are now facing the emotion of it, sometimes without realizing why. Others, totally unaware of reincarnation, are experiencing incidents in their lives that convince them they are going crazy. Many individuals locked in institutions have experienced such releases of energy.

"Life is but a play. When one goes back to glimpse a past life, it is just like a play in which he or she has been involved. The flashback is to release the painful suppressed energy of that particular life, so one may collect the fragment of his soul from that dimension of time and space and go on to better things. The awareness of what is happening will allow one totally to change his life for the better, by becoming more of a positive, outgoing, loving person."

This case history shows a common factor in many regressions: two individuals coming back and meeting each other again. What of other people now living with whom you have interacted in past lives? What of those long ago loves and hatreds that come back to haunt us now, demanding that amends be made or relationships fulfilled in order to work out our Karmic debt patterns?

Sometimes, regression is not even necessary. The "shock of recognition" can reawaken specific recall in two or more persons. And in this kind of meeting, past-life events *do* get "confirmed," by each individual's correcting and prompting the other.

I recently visited with Jane Roberts, author of the Seth books, and I asked for her thoughts regarding the flashbacks that most of us have experienced at one time or another—those sometimes fleeting, sometimes lengthy, sojourns to the past, containing what appear to be memories of some forgotten lifetime that are never attributable to this current life.

"I call these 'reincarnational dramas,'" Jane replied. "Many times they will be spontaneous with my students, with no prompting from me. A student will suddenly seem to be living an incident from a past life. Then another student will jump in, and before he realizes what is going on, we find that we have quite a drama going. I recall one example that involved a woman in her late forties and a young man in his late twenties. All of a sudden this lady began to act like a pioneer woman. She sat there in our group, wearing a long dress, with her legs out in front of her on the floor. You could have sworn she was holding a rifle in her lap."

According to Jane the woman suddenly cried out that the Indians were coming and said that her husband in that life had been quite a coward and would not fight to defend the family. She told of giving guns to the children and described how they fought off the attacking Indians. Throughout the reincarnational drama, the woman expressed a bitterness at her husband because he would not help protect his family.

"The young man in our class, it developed, had been the head of the Indian party that was attacking. We had about twenty in our class at the time, and suddenly I began to see this woman in my mind, squatting in the hut, with babies crying in the room.

"I did not want to get into the drama, for when emotions are flowing like that, I like to monitor. I just try to stay out of it and let them do their thing.

"As it developed, her husband in her present life was also her husband in that life.

"By the time everything was finished and the drama was over, Eleanor (my student) commented that whenever a conversation gets onto the subject of races or ethnic groups, she always sides with the Indians, despite her experiences in that past life. In some way, it seems that she and the Indians did eventually have some sort of reconciliation. The fight ended when the Indians realized that she had her problems and that all she really cared about were her children and defending them, and they ceased their attack."

Of course a skeptic would object that an ESP class would be just the environment to suggest a fantasy psychodrama. But the fact is, such "reincarnational dramas" often take place suddenly, in utterly nonstructured situations—and often, with many of the same lasting psychological benefits we've already cited.

# Chapter 6
## Other "Reincarnational Dramas"

Eric Jenson, a friend of mine who taught college for a number of years before leaving the halls of ivy for the business world, related a most interesting experience involving spontaneous recall of a past life:

"I taught economics, as you might guess. One semester I had a class in which three troublesome students seemed to block everything I tried to do. Oh, they weren't belligerent in a *Blackboard Jungle* sort of way, but they really seemed to be undermining my effectiveness in class by posing an endless number of irrelevant questions at odd moments. The three of them seemed to have a conspiracy against me.

"One day the three of them stayed after class. I was quite aware of them, but I chose to become terribly involved in cleaning the blackboard of some assignments I had written for the class to copy."

" 'Look at him,' Bob said. 'Just as damned imperious as ever. How arrogantly he turns his back on us!'

" 'Yes,' Charlie answered. 'He expects us to follow his orders implicitly, but he never stops to hear us out about our complaints.'

"'He'll have his moment of truth himself one day,' Pete said. All three of them were using stage whispers just loud enough to be clearly heard across the classroom.

"Look, you swabs!" I suddenly barked, turning on my heel. "If you had listened to me and followed my orders, then you wouldn't have been washed over to the sharks! A tropical storm is not a thing to be taken lightly!

"I had no idea why I had blurted out such a statement, and I felt very confused. I had always made it a point never to betray the slightest evidence of emotion in class. Why had I shouted such a ridiculous thing?

"If my verbal blast had disquieted me, the effect it had on my three students was incredible. They simply sat there with their mouths hanging open, and they became statue-still at their desks. As I looked at them at that moment, I saw them dressed in sailors' costumes of a time long past. And I seemed to be aware of captain's buttons on my blue suit.

"I was no longer in the classroom, or so it seemed. I was now on a storm-tossed sailing vessel, struggling to maintain some mastery of a violent sea. In several rapid flashes I saw myself as a stiff-backed British sea captain, harshly dealing out instant justice—as I saw it. Yet, at the same time, I saw myself as an individual who truly had his men's best interests foremost in consideration. It was necessary for a captain to be an unyielding pillar of strength in order to serve as the coalescing factor in holding the crew together during the long voyages.

"Then I clearly saw my three troublesome students in different guises, yet somehow recognizable. One was a junior officer, and the two others were common seamen who considered the officer's judgment above my own. The three of them had formed an almost mutinous conspiracy aboard ship, seeking to undermine my orders, inspiring incessant dissension among the crew. At last, in an act of desperation, I ordered the three men to be lightly flogged, then clapped in irons for a week. To treat a junior officer this way was to humiliate him beyond any point of reconciliation, but he had left me no choice.

"Shortly after their return to duty, our vessel was beset by a tropical storm. I shouted orders to everyone, carefully—albeit rapidly—issuing instructions on how best to survive the crisis. The three rebels set about following their own course of action and were swept overboard. Any attempt to reclaim them from the sea would have been futile and foolhardy.

"Dave, all of this came to me in an incredible kind of flash of memory and surprising recognition. I don't know how long I sat slumped behind my desk, but when I became conscious of the classroom once again, my three insurgents were still sitting there with their mouths open.

" 'Ah, Cap . . . er, ah, *Professor* Jenson,' one of them began, betraying the fact that he, at least, had undergone the same kind of strange revelatory experience.

"I cut him off, and I asked each of them to write down his impressions of the past few minutes and to take special care to detail any thoughts he might have had—regardless of how far out they might seem. For practically the first time that year, the three young men complied with my instructions. Amazingly, we found that our shared trance state, our reverie *en rapport,* produced internal dramas which agreed on all principal details.

"Now, Dave, you know that I simply am not into all of these things, so I still won't offer any explanations for what happened. I do know that the three young men and I had an entirely different relationship from that time on. We discussed the experience immediately afterward, but to my recollection, we never again mentioned the episode. I think we all felt a little awkward, a bit embarrassed by the extraordinary experience.

"But we had shared something which all four of us believed was meaningful on some level of being. None of us was able to interpret it, but on a personal level I became more concerned with my students' welfare. And my three rebels became—if not exactly model students—much more thoughtful and considerate."

An author and lecturer whom I'll call Rachael told me of the time when she was waiting for a professor who was to take her to the airport to catch the connecting flight to her next lecture engagement.

"The professor, Larry, and I had hit it off really well. He had been extremely helpful during my stay at the small New England college. I had my suitcases packed and I was skimming through a magazine when I heard his knock at the door.

"I am a bit over five-foot-seven, and Larry was only five-eight, so I was used to looking eye-to-eye at him. When I opened the door, I saw Larry, but now he stood at least six feet tall! And then his face was not Larry's—and yet it was. I began to feel terribly disoriented, dizzy, nauseated. I slumped back to the room and stretched out on the floor. For all the world, I felt as if I were having labor pains!

"Larry was instantly solicitous, and I reached out for him. The hotel room just melted away. I was lying on a crude bed in what I knew was France, probably sometime in the mid-1700's. I was in childbirth, experiencing excruciating pain, and from the look of the harried midwife's grim countenance, things were not going well.

"I heard a voice that I knew to be my mother's sobbing: 'She is dying, and she is nothing more than a baby herself. Where is Alain now that she needs him so?'

"The accusing question was directed toward my husband, who was absent from my bed of pain and travail. I, too, began to cry out for Alain.

"In a rush of images I saw how we had married as teenagers against our parents' protests. I was only a girl of sixteen, and the baby within me, the fruit of our love's union, was killing me.

"Then I gave a shudder and lay still. I was dimly aware that I had died. Larry later said that it seemed as though I had stopped breathing and that my pulse had become virtually nonexistent.

"At that point, he was swept with panic. He clutched me in his arms and began to sob: 'Marie, I loved you so. It wasn't my fault that I was not there at your bedside. I had gone to get the bottle of medicinal herbs and was on my way home, but some men provoked me into a fight. I was badly beaten, and I did not get home until two days after you were dead. I was grief-stricken. I never married, do you hear me? I never married again. I love only you!"

"Larry sobbed these things as if in a trance. He said later that he was somehow aware of what he was saying, yet at the same time was hearing them as if someone else were speaking the lines.

"After his tearful proclamation of love for me, I began to feel very much better. I was able to help Larry out of his stunned state of mind, and we sat for a long time talking in my hotel room. I missed my flight, but at that moment it seemed very unimportant.

"Larry had never experienced such a thing, and he was somewhat distraught. I have always had an openness to these kinds of experiences, so we sat there carefully trying to analyze what we both felt was somehow a sacred moment.

"We had both experienced the same imagery, it seemed, and had felt a thorough identification with the personalities of Alain and Marie. As rational as we both tried to be about the episode, none of the explanations we were able to devise made any more sense than the frank statement that at one time we had lived in France as husband and wife. One level of ourselves had recognized those residual lives and had a keen awareness of the unresolved sorrow and pain. It was somehow necessary that that aspect of me that was still Marie receive that kind of profession of love and faithfulness from that aspect of Larry that was still Alain. That aspect of my soul, or whatever, needed to hear from Larry/Alain's own lips why he had not been present at Marie's death bed.

"Larry made arrangements for another flight. He was a bachelor and I was at that time divorced, but romantics will be disappointed to learn that the two souls did not once again unite in blissful love. There had been that one intense moment of recognition, followed by the emotional release of past memories. After that, the information seemed to have registered properly. All deeper issues appeared to have been resolved in a manner deemed satisfactory to the levels of self involved. Although we have kept in touch by letter, we have never seen each other again."

A young man who prefers to be called Matt is a highly successful editor with a major East Coast publishing company. I first met him through our mutual friend and associate, Brad Steiger. When I mentioned that I was doing a new book on reincarnation, Matt agreed to share his past-life regression experience. Being a believer that nothing happens by pure chance, I was not surprised.

After Matt had provided me with his side of the story, I asked Brad if he would mind sharing some of his own impressions. He read over the account that Matt had sent me, chuckled in a few places, then also agreed to comment. Whatever power-behind-the-scenes prevailed, he and Brad were eventually drawn together through past-life Karmic structures dating to ancient times. Matt recounted:

"I first met Brad Steiger in the lobby of the Hotel Algonquin in New York City to go over some book ideas. Now when two strangers with a mutual interest in the occult get together, there's usually a quick camaraderie, a sharing of experiences, yarns, and even opposing philosophies. The tacit recognition that both are prowling around areas not quite respectable engenders a gentle humor. But what surprised me was that Brad seemed almost relentlessly professional, observing me intently, seemingly waiting for me to answer some question.

"From what I know of him now, this behavior seems especially strange, but back then I had nothing else to go on. Being a young editor, I was used to having older authors look down their noses at me, so I shrugged it off. The book we had discussed, about a buddy of his, didn't work out. But I contracted him for another project, and we fell into the close letter-and-telephone contact that authors and editors should.

"But our personal relationship still remained formal. I had the feeling that some aspect of my behavior just didn't sit right with him. Every once in a while Brad would slip some moral precept into our conversations, but what *was* odd was my reaction to it. I'm fairly easy-going, but I found that I resented Brad's unspoken implications in the worst possible way. Again, with hindsight, I realize I was reacting not to the specific present situation, but to his *role*. This is something I've seen again and again when I first meet someone from a past life: it's like seeing a movie starring an actor you've seen in previous films. You recall his performance in an earlier flick, and can't really accept his new screen characterization."

"I eyed Matt so strangely during that first meeting because he had some spinach stuck between his front teeth," Brad teased. "No, Matt was most presentable, but he was so irritatingly familiar—though I knew that I had never seen him before. I do a great deal of lecturing, and I become weary of people who play the reincarnation game. You know, those people who rush up after the lecture and say, 'Don't you remember when I bested you in the mungo tournament on Atlantis?' If I deny such a recall, they walk away in a huff, announcing to all within earshot that I certainly am not very tuned-in after all. But Matt wasn't playing that game at all.

"At the same time, of course, I suppose nearly everyone has experienced that sensation of instant like—or dislike—when he meets a total stranger. In some cases, there truly does seem to be a heavy rush of memories associated with the new friend. Psychologists might argue about projection or associations with mustaches, crooked teeth, bushy eyebrows, or some such thing that triggers memories from early present-life encounters. But some meetings do seem to be immediately provided with lengthy psychic dossiers. When I first met Matt, my internal computer banks seemed to go wild.

"I really had no idea that I was coming off so stuffy, moralistic, and judgmental with Matt. But, again, as Matt says, he may have been reacting more toward his past associations with me—if we did indeed receive a true unfoldment of a past life. Whatever triggered the associations, it certainly involved a number of factors."

Matt continued:

"But Brad and I are—always have been—gentlemen, and so everything remained at a private and personal level. Then, quite spontaneously, I began having most disquieting dreams about crucifixion—not *the* Crucifixion, but the general mode of death.

"Even now, I'm extraordinarily sensitive on the whole subject. Often I'll say 'when Christ *was killed,*' in search of an euphemism. I always wince at sick Easter jokes, and even the most innocuous cross metaphors in movies or theatre give me genuine distress. I've never been particularly religious, but now that my "cross" dreams were featuring me as the central figure, I began worrying that some religious hysteria might be bubbling up in my subconscious.

"I had long been a good friend of Jane Roberts, whose books, *The Seth Material* and *Seth Speaks,* give only a brief glimpse of the richness and variety of the ESP classes she was then holding each Tuesday night. I attended class about once or twice a year, and at one of these, during a break in the discussion, I asked Jane if odd death dreams could be simply remembrances from past lives.

"Immediately one of her star pupils, a warm and psychically gifted person named Sue, beckoned me aside and immediately tuned in on something. 'It was Yugoslavia,' she said to me, 'not Yugoslavia today, but when the Roman Empire was on the decline. You had been exiled there after something you did, when you were a scribe to a Roman governor. Now, with the Empire in chaos, the legions were undisciplined. A number of soldiers on the rampage came in and crucified a number of the village men. I see you in a cart, your hands tied, with several others, and they're driving you up a low hill . . .'

"Okay, okay. Stop right there!" I insisted. Not all of Sue's points seemed right, but I recalled enough to know I didn't want to remember the rest of that short journey.

"Later Sue wrote down her impressions for me, adding that she felt I was again acquainted with the Roman Governor in this life, and had a love-hate relationship with the individual. But none of those I felt mixed feelings for seemed to fit the description, so I let it drop. The dreams did stop, however.

"Then one day Brad called, and I noticed a radical change in his tone of voice. He seemed genuinely puzzled, searching for an answer he *didn't* know. He mentioned, half apologetically, that he had dreamed of me in what seemed to be the South Seas, with palm trees around, and wondered if it was a past-life memory.

"I've never turned on to *Mutiny on the Bounty*, so I asked him how I'd been dressed. 'Sort of a toga...' Brad said.

"Suddenly something clicked. I had never mentioned Sue's impressions or my dreams to him, but I went right ahead. 'Brad,' I asked evenly, 'Weren't you the Roman Governor?'

"I've seldom heard Brad at a loss for words, but there was a *long* pause at the other end of the line. I filled him in only briefly on Sue's reading, and we agreed that each of us would try to recall what we could independently, and then compare notes."

Brad then recalled:

"In fragmentary dreams which I had at that time, I saw myself as a rather stocky, middle-aged man, who, I must say, carried himself with great dignity and authority. I further saw myself in Egypt—at first I was aware only of the date trees, which I interpreted as 'palm trees,' thus making the earlier South Seas identification—receiving distressing news about an entity I knew was Matt. I also knew that I was Roman, an individual with certain influence, very much devoted to my city and my Emperor. The Empire was being invaded by hordes from the north, and it seemed that betrayal, deceit, and corruption constituted the order of the day. Now I had received news that a trusted scribe, a young man I regarded as a son, had also been accused of traitorous activities.

"Another dream saw me in Rome, seated resolutely in a chair, manfully holding back my sorrow and disappointment. Matt claimed to have been unjustly accused. He stood before me bound, trussed up between two guards. He was tall,

slender, and had reddish blond hair.* (In this life, Matt and I
are almost exactly the same height, and he has dark hair, as I
do. I may have been studying him somewhat suspiciously
because he didn't look as he should.) I wanted to believe him,
but the evidence seemed to damn him beyond pardon. I used
my influence to have him exiled, rather than executed."

Matt continued:

"Later that day I took a piece of paper and tried to get down
what I thought my name might have been. The first syllable
that came to me was 'dron,' and others seemed just to fit on
either side. I kept repeating the name under my breath and
editing and correcting it until it seemed right. Phonetically,
what I'd written was 'Seelhyas Haudronikoi.'

"I had nearly flunked Latin in school, and had never
studied any other ancient language, but I did know that Greek
was the diplomatic language in Roman times, just as French
was in the 1800's. So I submitted my piece of paper to another
editor who had studied ancient languages, including Greek.

" 'Seelhyas doesn't mean anything,' he said, 'but the last
word is the Greek genitive form. So you could translate it as
'Seelhyas of Houndronikos.'

" 'Haundronikos,' " I corrected him. It made perfect sense.
Up to medieval times, last names were infrequent, and people
were often known as Catherine of Sierma, Geoffrey of Mon-
mouth, and so forth.

"Brad called later that week, and said that, meditating, he
had gotten my name as 'Celos.' Yet even this discrepancy made
sense. A native Dalmation would of course 'remember' his
given name according to local pronunciation, but his Roman
superior would probably Hellenize it into the closest Greek
equivalent. Even in *this* life, people often transpose my name to
a form they're more used to.

"Brad now recalled, too, why he had felt concerned enough

---

*Sue's account had described Seelhy as just this way.

to mention his toga-and-palmtree dream. In his dream, he knew I was being killed; and while he felt partly responsible, he was powerless to stop it! I assured him it *wasn't* his fault, of course. Hearing the rest of Sue's story, he gratefully agreed with me."

Brad pointed out:

"I'm certain, Dave, that you have noted the reversal in our roles today. In a real sense, I, as an author, am a scribe for Matt, who as editor, governs certain aspects of my work. Again, I cannot deny that our psyches might have devised such a framework in order to promote a camaraderie in our working relationship.

"It cannot be overlooked, though, that we were over a thousand miles apart when we each came up with similar data, including names and descriptions. If our psyches creatively conspired to produce such a mechanism, then time and space certainly do not pose the kind of barriers to unity which we have been taught."

Matt added:

"Since our mutual discovery, Brad and I have become infinitely closer and truly good friends. But what still amuses me is my recollection that as his scribe, I was somewhat too big for my toga, and even stepped out of it once for a fling with the woman who was then Brad's wife! He can't seem to recall that part of the saga, but even that makes sense. If the woman— who was *not* the same entity as Brad's current wife Marilyn— didn't mean all that much to him, he would have forgotten her more easily than I did. And yet, Dave, now *he* recalls a life in which *he* was the adulterous lover.

"Anyway, I would have to discount this lascivious detail as possible fantasy on my part if I hadn't run into that errant matron, again in the flesh, and been able to recall incidents and details that meshed exactly. But that's another story. Still, the first time I met Brad, he was with his 'present'—and only—wife Marilyn, and perhaps that explains why he was watching me so closely."

# Chapter 7

## Charting Your Own Past Journeys

Perhaps in the final analysis, we must all ask ourselves: What is practical? Have I lived before, and have those many lives before this one served any purpose in the present scheme of things?

There is nothing we can do to undo events of the past. But the fact that we are powerless to change the past need not imply that it cannot continue to serve the present. Every event of the past, in this and previous lifetimes, can and must serve a need today, for they are responsible for what we are this very minute.

This does not mean that we must brood over past errors or revel in glories, but there are certain lessons that each phase of life serves, and the sum total of a past life must serve a purpose in this one.

There is an old saying that if something is neither useful nor ornamental, we should get rid of it. A rose is beautiful, but serves little purpose beyond being ornamental. The anvil has little esthetic value, but its usefulness is beyond question when hammering metals. Each has its purpose and serves a practical need.

No subject is worth studying if it does not have a practical value. No one spends years learning to be a lawyer unless he plans either to become a practicing attorney or to use that knowledge in the fields of business or politics. How, then, can we figure past lives at less value than we would a single lifetime career? Even though we may not be able to gain more than brief glimpses of those past lives, their effect is deep-seated in the subconscious and unconscious levels of us all.

Every individual's life is dependent upon others. Just as we must depend from time to time on other people within our social structure, so we must at times depend upon those "other people" we have been in times past. What we were, did, and thought long ago remains with us to this very minute. You are you because of who you were in a variety of roles played long ago. You will always retain a certain element of the philosopher, the warrior, the royalty, or the serf; and through association with those past incarnations you become a better person today, for you have the capacity to empathize with those around you. You have been among the wealthy as well as the ghetto-dwellers. You have been the prisoner as well as the freeman. You have served in high places as well as the low realms of one society or another. The lessons learned at many levels are serving you in this lifetime, whether or not you are cognizant of the fact.

So in order to make our present lives practical we must depend at times on the lessons and experiences gained during past incarnations. You have seen now how various individuals have gained insights to the past through altered states of consciousness and an awareness of the fleeting "memories" we all experience from time to time. Your fear of water or fire, those splitting headaches, the chronic abdominal pains, the natural ability to paint, the gift of prophecy, music, or acting, empathy for the underdog, the love of humanity—are they purely accidental, or could they have a higher meaning? Are you just lucky, or could it be that you have earned the rewards you seem to be reaping in this life? Or are you asking, "Why me, God? What did I do to deserve the horrible fate you have handed me?"

Perhaps it is time to look within, to examine seriously the prospect that your fate—good, bad, or so-so—is the direct result of what you were and what you did to others or *for* others in past lives. With the help of some highly qualified people, I will present various ways to realize your potential. We are discovering what techniques are employed by various practitioners in this field, including self-realization, hypnosis, and meditative methods. But regardless of what outside help you may need to get started, in the final analysis it will be you who make the final decisions that will benefit your daily living.

Those who are accomplished in the field of reading past lives for others can help direct their clients in the paths that will give practical meaning to events of past lives which can serve as guiding influences in their present incarnations. I am still open to the idea that certain gifted individuals can effectively help others, and can serve as valuable guides for the individual. Yet I feel it is highly improbable that a reincarnational reading carried out by a total stranger at some remote area, via the U.S. mail, can be as effective as a life reading conducted in person, where a psychic sensitive has a chance to tune into the individual.

"Send your name, date of birth, birthplace, and $15 to Madam Ziltch for a past-life reading."

Your $15, plus equal amounts from hundreds of equally gullible people, will make Madam Ziltch wealthy eventually, but it is doubtful that it will give you a true insight to any of your past lives. Often, those doing the mail order readings send out a questionnaire in which they gain information about family members, present occupation, and the like. It is a simple thing to then say that your present wife was your daughter in ancient Greece or that you are a writer today because you were a scribe in Rome, and so forth. While such statements could be true, they do stretch credulity a bit, if for no other reason than they really don't say anything that could not be an educated guess. Furthermore, they say very little that can truly benefit the individual interested in learning past details in order to rebuild his present life into one that is more satisfactory. I have seen several such readings and can only say that they contain more "guessages" than messages, and offer more than a little confusion to the serious student of reincarnation.

As in all matters, let the buyer beware. Do not jump into a trap simply because an advertisement in a publication tells what a great past-life reader a certain person may be. Remember, he paid for the ad and can pretty well say what he wants to about himself. "Investigate before you invest"'applies here. If you must depend on the mail order life readings of a stranger, at least be sure you know something of that individual's credentials. How has he helped others of your personal acquaintance? Does he give a message that has depth to it? Does he strike certain chords of familiarity with others, indicating that he might do the same for you?

I believe the probings of dreams and meditation are more productive. The revelations that you gain through dreams, meditation, and the alpha zone or hypnogogic stage seem to be best, for they are more personal.

One thing that must be underlined is the body of teachings that tell us the Kingdom is within, not in some far-off heavenly location—the fundamentalist concept that has managed to turn off many people today. When we turn within, we should find, among other things, inner peace, calmness, and tranquility. Also, we find that ancient bookkeeping system called the Akashic Record: our own personal record not only of events from this incarnation, but of who we were, what we did, and why we did it in *every* lifetime.

Various altered states of consciousness can serve as valuable tools to make contact with previous incarnations.

The case of Jack McCord of Canton, Ohio, can serve as a good survey of the various attitudes and "do it yourself" techniques.

I was rummaging through my research files one day when my eye was caught by a letter from Jack McCord telling of his incarnation during World War I as the British flying ace Albert Ball. I immediately told myself that I must contact this man.

Within a few days I received a cordial letter from McCord along with some regression material concerning his alleged life as the famed aerial ace credited with downing more than 40 German planes.

"My current life as Jack McCord began on October 31, 1921, in Nebraska, although we soon moved to Ohio. I can remember the deep yearning inside me to one day be a pilot. Then when I saw my first movie about the First World War's fighter pilots, I knew that I had literally been there.

"I can remember the times I spent in my bedroom at the foot of the old iron bed, which was my imaginary plane that I flew to shoot down the enemy. I knew just what to do in order to maneuver my plane, and I would work my hands and feet on my controls in a proper manner. I was always filled with an enormous amount of energy, and I was extremely happy. I would often find myself going to the airports, moving from hangar to hangar, watching the planes take off. I experienced a great desire to be in those planes.

"Through my teen years, my eyes gradually weakened, and I was told that I could not be a pilot. I became totally disillusioned with life, for this was a terrible blow to my ego. Following the attack on Pearl Harbor—and my twenty-first birthday—I went into the Army, despite the ever-present yearning to be a pilot.

"After returning from the Central Burma Campaign, I returned to Ohio and came across a childhood buddy of mine who encouraged me to enlist in the Ohio State Guard. I was eventually promoted to the rank of captain.

"One day, after reading a book written by a noted psychic, I found myself admiring this man and his work. I had felt a reawakening of my soul. The subject of reincarnation fascinated me beyond explanation, and I became aware that in the near future I would experience something new. The idea of reincarnation really puzzled me, because this belief was not obvious in the Bible, a book I am quite familiar with. I read some books on reincarnation, and I discovered how to manifest a vision of a past lifetime. Periodically, at night, I would attempt this experiment.

"One night I drifted into a deep sleep, and during that sleep I had a vision of myself dressed in the uniform of a pilot, wearing a leather jacket and boots, a helmet, and goggles. The body was that of a young and powerful man. In the vision there were three or four of us who had just landed at an air base. We were cold and hungry, so we went to dinner. Laughing and clowning around, I was approached by someone who asked me who I was. I told him that I was English, but as I started to give my name, I woke up. Having a pencil and pad beside my bed, I got up to record the incident.

"The next day I was confused about what had occurred in my sleep the night before. Having been reared by a Western family and taught a set way of life, in a strict religion, it was hard for me to change at this late date when I discovered that there was more to life than I had been told. Finding that I had lived another life on Earth was jarring: It was in contrast to all I had been taught.

"I decided to work the Ouija board to see if I could get any answers to my questions. Immediately, the board began to tell me that I had been Albert Ball and that I had flown in World War I. I had never heard of this man before. The thought then occurred to me that I might be able to do automatic writing.

"Holding a pencil in my hand and sitting completely relaxed, my hand began to move. Scribbling and doodling at first, my writing gradually progressed to where I could unmistakably see the words, 'You and I are one.' I then questioned myself by asking who it was that I had made contact with. The script answered, 'Albert Ball' and it went on to tell me that I had flown in the First World War.

"Curious to know who Albert Ball had been, I asked for information on this man. The pencil wrote that he had been an English pilot of World War I. Ball had flown a late model airplane and had 43 German planes to his credit.

"During the next few days I went about deeply absorbed in all that had been happening. Each night I would go to bed with these thoughts on my mind.

"One night, after a hard day's work, I was so tired that I went directly to bed and I drifted off almost instantly. I saw a screen open before my eyes. On this screen, I first saw a German plane going down, in flames. Next I found myself slipping into the body of the man who was in the cockpit of the higher plane. I was firing from the mounted guns at a German plane, and I could see the shots I fired going into the engine of the enemy plane. I saw the plane burn and fall.

"All of a sudden into my own cockpit came a stream of bullets, penetrating my instrument panel. The plane was moving upward, turning to the left. I suddenly felt as though I was no longer in the cockpit. I felt myself drifting out of the body. I could see the British emblem on the top wing of the plane I had just left. I could see the plane drifting off . . . . As the plane drifted away, I was awakened. As before, I recorded the incident.

"About two weeks later my aunt and uncle were going on vacation and asked me to check on their house during their absence. A few days after they had gone, an inner guiding force told me to visit my nephew, Gary Rossetti. When I got to his house, I asked him if he would care to go along with me to my aunt's house. To my surprise, he told me that he knew that I was coming to see him.

"As we arrived at my aunt's house, Gary said that he had felt a presence around him. Placing ourselves in a receptive frame of mind, we began to bring through psychic impressions from my subconscious mind. As Gary began to receive more impressions, which he wrote down, he became convinced that the communications were not from a separate entity, but from my own soul. I remained quiet and allowed him to continue writing down information.

"Through psychic union with my mind, Gary received the following impressions of the personality of Albert Ball: (1) he was headstrong, very determined, keen-minded, and quick-to-action; (2) he was husky and powerfully built; (3) he excelled mainly along military lines; (4) he was very strong, although it was picked up, impressionally, that he had either a scar on his left knee or an injury on this knee; (5) he had much artistic ability and, for a brief time, had played the violin; (6) he died near the age of 20 or 21, from a gunshot, which entered in the lower left side of the back of his head, near his left ear; (7) the personalities of Jack McCord and Albert Ball seemed, at times, inseparable; (8) Ball had not had a wife; (9) he had been flying a new model plane when he was shot; and (10) when he passed into the next world, he was in a state of shock. Those are not all the impressions received, but they were those that stood out above the others.

"Gary and I both went to psychics to see whether or not the impressions received were genuine or mere wishful thinking. We were convinced that they were true and also that we both possessed powers within us that were only now coming to the fore ... but will be developed in time, through patience and understanding."

Jack McCord further reported that he has had regression readings from a number of well-known psychics, who have confirmed his World War I incarnation as Albert Ball, as well as several other past lives that he discovered through meditation over the years. William J. Finch of Phoenix, Arizona, using the pendulum technique,* also confirmed that McCord and Albert Ball are one and the same individual. The Reverend and Mrs. Werefield, Spiritualist ministers of Cleveland, Ohio, during a seance said, "I see the spirit of Albert Ball entering the body of Jack McCord at birth."

McCord attended a lecture by Dr. Douglas Baker of England, who underlined the belief that quite often when a person meets sudden death, the entity returns in a short time to take up another life. This opinion satisfied McCord as to why he had been born again so soon after the war years.

McCord related the impressions he received, during meditation, of the emotions felt by Albert Ball immediately following his death:

*The pendulum technique involves the use of a small object, such as a crystal ball or other weighted object, suspended on a light chain or string. The pendulum is then positioned over a sheet of paper containing the words "yes" and "no" in the form of a cross. If the pendulum swings in the direction of "yes" — say up and down, then the answer is affirmative, etc.

"Where am I? Where am I? What is wrong with me? I am no longer in my plane. How is this possible? Am I dead? No, I can't be; I'm still conscious. I must be dead because I can see my plane falling, but what or where am I? I must be dreaming. Where is everyone else? Maybe I've been captured, and they've drugged me. No, I can't believe what is going on. Where am I, how did I get here? I can't remain here without falling. Help! Help! Can anyone hear me? Please help me. Am I dead? My head is bleeding. Anyone, someone, can you hear me? Somebody please help me. Where am I? My plane, my plane. What's happened to me? What's wrong with me? I must be mad. This war has gotten to me, that must be it. Help me, someone. Where am I? I'm mad; those damn Germans did this to me! Wait 'til I get back from wherever I am. We must win this war. What's going on? No one can see me. It's as if I'm invisible. Someone, help me, please. Those damn Germans! Those damn Germans! My plane. Got to get to my plane. My head. Where am I? Help me. My plane, my plane . . . ."

It is not possible to prove beyond doubt that Jack McCord and Albert Ball are one and the same, but research into the life of Albert Ball did reveal that he was indeed a Royal Flying Corps "ace" of World War I, credited with downing 43 German planes, and that he was killed by German snipers who mounted a machine gun on top of a clock tower in the Flemish village of Annoeullin, where Ball had the habit of buzzing the tower on his return from sorties over Germany. There is some conflict as to his age, however. *The Doughboys* by Lawrence Stallings claims Ball was 19 when killed. *Dictionary of National Biography (1912-1921)* agrees with McCord's statement that Ball was 21 at the time of his death. The latter reference also states that Ball was killed when he flew into a formation of three German planes, led by Manfred Freiherr, and that Ball shot down two of those planes before being killed by the third.

Whichever account is accurate, the fact remains that Albert

Ball did indeed live and fight in World War I. The only important question remaining is: Are Albert Ball and Jack McCord one and the same, or has some quirk of fate endowed McCord with a certain psychic ability to pick up the thought waves of the long dead Albert Ball?

We may well be the result of our past incarnations, as evidenced by the effect that Albert Ball has had on the present incarnation of Jack McCord. McCord realizes that the personality of Albert Ball was one of extended ego. He feels that as McCord he was born into a fresh life just three years after the demise of Ball in order to stabilize his personality, since in this current incarnation he has devoted his efforts to helping others as a hypnotist and as a teacher of meditation techniques. Certain memories have instilled in McCord the early desire to be a flyer, and the later interest in military subjects that remain with McCord to this day. There was, however, a more profound influence in that McCord, in this life, feels the urgency to relay his metaphysical beliefs, to devote his present incarnation to one of sharing, as opposed to the ego-centered life experienced as Albert Ball.

McCord is finding a soul-satisfaction in his work as a hypnotist and a teacher of meditative techniques, a role he would probably never have played if it were not for those revelations years ago concerning rebirth and his former lives, especially the one as Albert Ball.

# Chapter 8

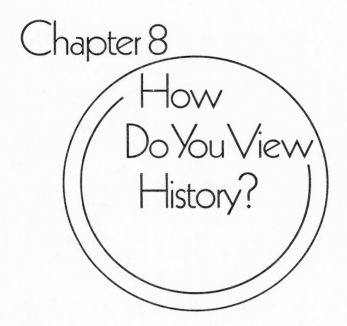

## How Do You View History?

It is doubtful that any two people out of ten view history in exactly the same way. Some look at history as the normal progression of man in his constant endeavor to find the elusive Utopia. Others may accept past events with the same emotions that they show toward a dramatic program on television—for edification or simply to be enjoyed for the moment, but of no concern beyond information or escapism.

To many, however, history has a certain familiarity or point of identity—not all history, of course, but certain eras, certain specific points in man's progress. To many of us, perhaps yourself included, there are bits and pieces of mankind's past that are a bit too vivid to ignore—almost like memories.

How do you view history? Think about it for a while; it could make all the difference in the world to you, for in the past lies the key to the present and future. If this is not the first time around, you and I and everyone else have been on this particular plane of existence before.

Some time ago I visited with Lee R. Gandee, author of *Strange Experience* (Prentice-Hall, 1971), and he commented on his views of history and how he feels they have had a direct effect on his current incarnation. Lee mentioned that for some unknown reason he has always had an uneasy feeling about the Catholic Church, a feeling that seemed inborn, for he has no reason to be at odds with Catholicism, based on events of this life.

"I met a student at Lenoir Rhyne whom I recognized instantly," Lee told me. "I knew that he was an associate from a former life, and that we had been in the midst of a religious persecution. In that lifetime I had lost my wife, home, and children, and eventually my life, because of the authority of the Catholic Church."

He and his friend could both recall every family member, men, women, and children, being killed by men with crossbows after having been taken into the mountains above their burning village. He had the feeling that this event took place at the time of the Salzburg persecution in Austria. Later, after gaining additional insight into that incarnation, he decided it must have been during the Hussite movement in Bohemia, in the fifteenth century.

"I feel this persecution as strongly as if it were in my present life, happening to my present family. This strong emotional feeling is directed against the royal family of Hapsburg as much as it is against the Catholic Church."

Such a recall of history, as unpleasant as it may be, can serve the pragmatic scheme by allowing the individual to realize that there is no justification for retaining present hatreds and prejudices, since these events happened long ago to another personality.

Preferences for certain styles of art may be a good clue to tastes you may have acquired at the time. The young editor called Matt has been told he was also a monk in thirteenth-century France. When he visited an exhibition of stained glass at New York's Metropolitan Museum, his eye immediately "chose" one panel as superior to all the others. It was the only example in the show dating from thirteenth-century France!

When I was a youngster living in Elmhurst, Illinois, my fifth-grade teacher formed a science club. I was much interested in science, especially astronomy, and I was eager to join. As it turned out, when I reached junior high school, the teacher transferred to the same school, so our science club lasted for a full four years.

During those years we took monthly field trips to various points of interest around Chicago, including the Brookfield Zoo, the Museum of Science and Industry, and Field Museum. It was the trips to Field Museum that intrigued me most, for each time we entered the Egyptian Rooms, I had a feeling that I was "back home." Now, at that early age I had never heard of the idea of reincarnation and would have certainly laughed at the thought. Although at age seven I had started questioning all religious philosophies, my thoughts at that time had not touched the rebirth hypothesis.

Yet, for some unexplained reason, as the rest of the class passed on to other exhibits at the museum, I would on each visit remain for the rest of the day in the Egyptian section, viewing the mummy cases, the ancient artifacts, and hiero-glyphics. It was some years later that I visited Chicago and took in the rest of the world-famous Field Museum, but I still paused briefly "in Egypt." If reincarnation is a fact, and we have lived many lives before, then it is reasonable that at one time or another we could have lived in such population centers as Egypt, Greece, and China. Considering the length of time covered by the histories of these ancient civilizations, we could all have lived in each of them several times, and probably been on the social ladder from slave to royalty.

If you feel a certain "warmth" for one period in history, you will probably find that that era represents a life of growth and happiness—a lifetime when you truly accomplished something worthwhile. There may be other times that send cold chills up your spine. These obviously were less-than-pleasant lifetimes, but there are certain lessons to be learned from them as well. The sooner you get on the past-life path, the sooner you will find episodes that will alleviate certain fears or will help you promote certain talents and abilities.

Jack McCord's story had a particular appeal to me, due to my own revelations concerning a past life as a World War I fighter pilot. Another "memory" of mine goes back to my earliest years as a youngster in this present life. There were still many biplanes flying our skies, but nothing in this early period could account for the feeling of closeness to that era which ended nine years before my present life began.

One day, in the late 1930's, I went to the airport at Elmhurst, and there rested a World War I vintage biplane. I walked up to it, looked in, and once again got the feeling that I was "back home." I climbed into the cockpit and *knew* that I could fly that plane without one bit of trouble! Thank God, there was no other equally confident youngster around to crank the propeller for me, or I might have proved my theory—or disproved it, as the case may be.

Still more years passed before I was able to tie this particular feeling into a past-life recall that revealed, at least to my satisfaction, that I had indeed served in World War I as a flyer until my death in a flaming dogfight in 1918.

The meditative vision itself shows me in the cockpit of a World War I plane—believed to be a Spad—in pursuit of a German plane, amid the sound of machine guns. Suddenly, without warning, the cockpit of my plane became a blazing inferno—and that was it! That was my last memory of my incarnation as a fighter pilot of World War I.

Later revelations showed more details of that life, which serve little purpose here. I was not a great war hero, just a simple pilot with a single mission of downing as many enemy planes as I could. I did find in my probings that there were several planes to my credit; and as I later pieced my story together with bits of information Brad Steiger had located, we came to the conclusion that Brad had been one of my victims in the skies east of France those many years ago.

It may seem odd to pay off a Karma involving killing in one life with a strong friendship and business association in another, but often the ways of Karma are beyond the comprehension of the mortal mind. But the World War I episode, or incarnation, if you will, tied in pragmatically with a long-time fear of my own that I would eventually die in a flaming plane crash. Obviously, I thought that this represented precognition, and I refused to travel by air for a number of years, taking the slower but "safer" trains, and driving when business necessitated travel. The regression relieved this anxiety, and I have since logged hundreds of happy and carefree hours aboard commercial planes, with the accompanying reduction of travel time— and the absence of fear.

A distinct inner awareness tells us that a particular emotion or feeling indicates some connection with a past life that is one of our very own—not the life of one we might read about in history books or experience vicariously through the printed page or electronic media, but a life we can touch upon through our own personal awareness, because *we were there!*

Marian B. from Rochester, New York, came to Ann Fisher for a reading. "At a certain point, she asked me about past lives, and I immediately tuned into a Roman lifetime. I felt she had been a Christian and had been killed by the lions in the Colosseum. The woman looked at me and became terrified. She said, 'But, how did you know?'

"She then said, 'I took a trip to Rome three years ago. When I went into the Colosseum and looked into the arena, I became terrified. I had this feeling that I had to leave. I ran all the way out. Ann, I believe it! I was thrown to the lions in the Colosseum during ancient times.'

"She continued: 'You know, it was so vivid that I told my friends about it. Of course, the ones who believe [in reincarnation] accepted it, and the others weren't sure about me!'

"I feel that anytime a past life comes through which has been connected with tragedy, the person will feel it strongly, he will have this remembrance. If it was a good time, he will also feel this as joy. Revisiting an actual place will bring back memories like nothing else."

Ann Fisher related a spontaneous regression of her own from a past life:

"I was in Houston, Texas, in 1971, and as I looked out the hotel window, I said to my husband, 'I see nothing but sagebrush.' If you were in downtown Houston and looked out of a hotel window, you would see nothing but parking lots! Suddenly, the parking lots did flash back in, and I realized that what I was seeing was a past life—that I had been there before. The place did seem familiar, and during age regression under hypnosis I picked up that I was Hungarian, had married an American, and moved to Texas in 1825. I stayed there, had two sons, but did not like the wilderness, the country, or the prairie, and eventually moved back to my native Hungary when I was in my forties. I was later killed in an accident."

Another alternative to the reincarnation concept that we must consider here is the idea of delusions of memory. We might be prone to take certain stories from childhood that we overheard from adults, then unknowingly adopt them to ourselves as the years pass, eventually giving "evidence" that we were reborn into another body, since these events obviously happened many years before our present incarnation began.

I recall vividly tales told by my father, uncles, and grand-fathers which fascinated me when I was probably no more than five or six years old. I have, to the best of my knowledge, been able to keep these events separated from my own personal memories. However, there is always the possibility that a few slipped by me and now account for what I might consider my own memories from another life.

The most recent lifetime that I can recall would be the World War I episode in which I was possibly a fighter pilot. Could this be the interchange of memory from one of my immediate ancestors? A delusion? I rather doubt it.

My father was too young for World War I. Although he tried to join the Navy when he was seventeen, he was prevented from doing so by his father, who refused to sign the necessary papers. Both uncles were still younger. My grandfathers, on the other hand, were both over the draft age. No war stories here.

I did have two second cousins who saw action in that war, but both were in the Army, and only one actually got to France. No other relatives served in World War I battles, so they obviously provided no war stories to fire my imagination.

Even though I cannot relate to such events in my own history, I do not discount the possibility that in some cases such delusions of memory or personal association with the stories related by older relatives might be the basis for some past-life "memories."

There are some people who claim to have strong emotional ties to that mysterious lost continent known as Atlantis, which allegedly disappeared from the face of the earth some 12,000 years ago, before the beginning of our own epoch.

Tenny Hale is a psychic who is gaining fame not only in the West Coast area near her home in Beaverton, Oregon, but nationally as well. Tenny has her own TV show in Portland on the local ABC affiliate, and has appeared in various national publications in recent years with highly accurate predictions. She was quoted in *Other Dimensions' Predictions for 1973* by Glenn McWane, as well as other books dealing with prophecies. Tenny, a housewife and mother, has related a situation very close to home: the life reading of her son Larkey.

The boy, from early years, could not stand to have anyone touch his hands, and Tenny found it necessary to warn his teachers and babysitters against grabbing his hands when correcting him, as this caused the boy to go into a rage.

A point not known by the counselor and life reader to whom Tenny took Larkey is that the boy is a hemophiliac, and the problem of bleeding to death is always present in the thoughts of his mother, who knows that even a slight cut can be fatal to her son. The regressionist said that the entity now known as Larkey had been a scientist in Atlantis who discovered how to make human beings in test tubes—a scientific breakthrough that we are approaching today. The government of Atlantis had a ruling Council, apparently, that determined the advisability of releasing certain scientific information, and when the entity told the Council of his discovery, they said it should not be done. They forbade him to continue with his experiments.

He then told them that he already had performed some creations and did not intend to give up his great scientific discovery. When he insisted on continuing these experiments, the Council ordered his hands cut off.

Then, with his teeth, he ripped the bandages off and said that he would bleed to death. Those around him asked him not to do this, that it was suicide, but he answered, "Yes, but that's your loss, not mine. See now if you can get along without me!"

The reader then told Tenny that her son had been born in this life with a blood disease, which of course, he has. Tenny pointed out that her father was a geneologist. He had traced the family back several generations and found that hemophilia is not a genetic problem in the family on either side, and that Larkey is the first hemophiliac.

The trauma, presumably dating back to Atlantis, is so severe that it can at times cause this normally happy and carefree child to turn almost vicious if his hands are touched. Larkey's second grade teacher told Tenny that she must do something with the boy, that she could not go back to the classroom where he was, for fear he might kill her. When Tenny asked what Larkey had done to cause her great fear, she said that he had actually *done* nothing, but it was the way he looked at her that invoked the fear.

This same report was echoed by several babysitters, and the psychic counselor believes that what actually is happening is that Larkey is recognizing these people as former associates from Atlantis who were responsible for having his hands amputated. As a young child, not fully aware of his own past, he is subconsciously reflecting hatred of the action for which these entities were responsible thousands of years ago.

He has never done physical violence, but it is the way Larkey looks at people that scares them. Further investigation showed that in each case, when the child persisted in doing something he was told not to do, the older person—teacher or babysitter—had touched his hands, and this invoked the look that brought fear. As a baby, touching Larkey's hands would cause him to scream with severe fright, but later it brought on the silent forboding stare.

Tenny told Larkey of the reading and what it disclosed, and he admitted that when he meets certain people he immediately, without knowing why, has a violent hatred and desire to kill them. As related by the reader, these people represent those who were his enemies long ago. Now that the basis of the problem has been found, and the Karmic structure accounted for, it will be interesting to see what results will eventually be realized in relation to his fear of having his hands touched and his instant hate for those he subconsciously recognizes as former antagonists.

Now there are ways to overcome the results of these past-life traumas. Of course Larkey must learn to forgive in order to alleviate the blocks in his own spiritual structure, brought forward into this life. Whether the hemophilia at this stage can be cured is questionable, but certainly it is not too late to overcome the fear of people touching his hands or the thoughts of killing others, which block his spiritual evolution.

This book does not concern itself with discussing the existence of lost continents such as Atlantis and Lemuria. But my research and interviews revealed many regressions into past lives that referred to Karmic debts formed during prior existences in Atlantis. If there were not so much present interest in this subject, I wonder if those lives might have had their origin in ancient Greece or Rome, for example. But Atlantis is the location often mentioned, so it is Atlantis with which we must deal.

Whether it be pure conjecture, mythology, or fact, the legends surrounding the famed lost continent of Atlantis come back at regular intervals to fire man's imagination. Many claim that Atlantis was technologically far in advance of our present scientific development. Television, jet airplanes, automobiles, space travel, and every conceivable marvel of our present day and many more were common to this great civilization. There are those who further claim that Atlantis was inhabited by philosophers who had discovered the riddles of the universe which plague our greatest minds today. In other words, that lost civilization can be summed up as the true example of a technological Utopia.

In all honesty we can neither endorse nor discount those who believe that Atlantis did exist at some point in our present pre-history. But nearly every known religion today has in its history the legend of the Great Flood or similar stories concerning a deluge and a complete inundation of its people. Could it be that all are referring to an epoch when in a single gigantic move the entire civilization slid into the depths of the ocean?

Suppose that a small handful of Atlantean travelers and merchants were in other countries when that happened. Perhaps in the backward countries of Egypt, India, Persia, or China, out of communication with their home bases. These travelers may have boarded their ships or jet planes and headed for home, only to find nothing but open water where Atlantis had been but a few days or weeks before. Then, completely confused, they would have returned to the only societies they knew still existed—the undeveloped countries where they had been when the tragedy took place. They would have had no choice but to assimilate into the remaining civilizations, muttering their stories about the homeland, the basis for later legends about lost Atlantis and how it vanished overnight.

To many in this time of the New Age, Atlantis is indeed a reality, and scientific evidence continues to pour in to substantiate the claims that a lost civilization did exist long ago, presumably in the Atlantic Ocean between the Americas and Europe-Africa. Recent discoveries indicate that a lost civilization—possibly Atlantis—is locked in the ice of Antarctica, the result of a great axis shift in antiquity that left this once-tropical land covered with hundreds of feet of ice. Fact or fantasy, we cannot at this point say for certain.

But it is not enough to view past lives objectively, for however spiritually evolved we may be, we are not advanced enough for complete objectivity. Our very presence in a current physical life suggests that we are still in need of earth-plane experiences. To fully benefit from past lives, you must learn to actually get into the emotional frame of consciousness and relive those past movements. You must become a part of the past in order to find the practical lessons presented in those former lives.

What were the emotions that made you what you were then? As you walked the earth long ago, what were the feelings that are still, at some emotional or mental level, affecting your life now? How do you truly relate to those "other persons" within? How do you gain insight that will take you back mentally and emotionally to those periods that shape your current self?

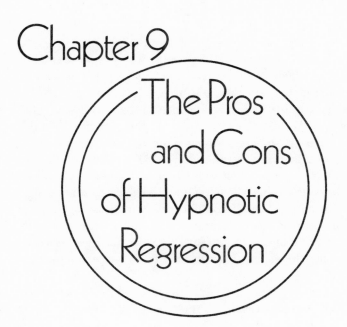

# Chapter 9
## The Pros and Cons of Hypnotic Regression

Dr. C. Norman Shealy feels that psychiatry is an absolute shambles. He says:

"I believe that psychoanalysis is utter nonsense. More people have been cracked up and wrung out in the name of the prurient interests of psychiatrists dabbling in the sexual extremes of their patients' lives than you can imagine.

"I don't believe that sex is the basis of most problems. There's no question that trouble between lovers, spouses, or what-have-you are extremely common and a major source of trouble, but to put it in terms of frank sex is not where it is.

"As far as I'm concerned, for people who have moderate to serious problems, the most useful technique is life regression. The simple neurotic doesn't need psychoanalysis or life regression; he can learn to balance himself with autogenic training and bio-feedback. The severely hung-up person or the psychotic needs something much more intense than that, and I believe that's where life regression could fill a tremendous role. I would *like* to see psychiatry aim in that direction, but I am not sure they are capable of making this kind of transition.

"We need psychiatrists to work with humanistic techniques, the best two of which I would consider life regression and autogenic training. I think Gestalt has its place and some of these other things, but I think really these two techniques are the best."

Hypnosis is gaining respect in the medical field today, and it has been used extensively in surgery as an anesthetic, as well as a method to probe the unconscious minds of patients undergoing psychiatric treatment.

Joseph De Louise came to national attention a few years ago with his work on the infamous Sharon Tate murder case. His predictions have been documented in *National Enquirer,* the *Chicago Tribune, Chicago Sun-Times, Other Dimensions' Predictions for 1973* by Glenn McWane, and numerous other publications, radio, and television broadcasts. Joe heads Mind Perfection Institute in Chicago.

A telephone call from my hotel room to the office of Joe De Louise resulted in an early appointment. I told Joe I was in Chicago to interview various psychics for my new book on reincarnation, and that I would appreciate a bit of his time for an interview. I knew that Joe is a busy psychic with a full schedule of appointments, so the best I was hoping for was a few minutes, perhaps a half hour *sometime* that week. It was

Tuesday morning, and I figured on four days to get the appointment.

"Fine, Dave, always glad to help. Where are you staying?"

"At the Bismark."

"Good!" I'll see you in five minutes, and we'll grab a cup of coffee!"

Sure enough, he was waiting for me when I got to his office, and our next stop was a coffee shop just down the street.

I had known of Joe's reputation as one of the nation's top psychics, but this was our first meeting. I knew, also, that Joe De Louise is no novice in the field of hypnosis and that he has done successful regressions in the past, so I opened the interview with some questions concerning his thoughts on hypnotic regression:

"More and more information is coming out through regression that makes reincarnation appear to be a fact, and we'll be seeing more of this work in the next couple of years, with more research going on.

"When I run up against a real stubborn case or some type of hangup that has no logical explanation in this person's life, I use hypnosis. I regress the client, hoping to go into a past life that will be meaningful. Many times it is very successful, and I find the hangup or the neurosis or the phobias from a past life that people carry into this life. It's very, very helpful to be able to do this, to locate the cause of the problem."

Joe feels we are going through a phase today in which it is a fad to try to find out something of what may be a past life recall through hypno-regression. He feels that we are evolving, however, to a point where more and more people are sincerely interested in learning more about themselves from a constructive standpoint, and abandoning the so-called ego-trips in which they are basically trying to find a past-life where they were a famous personage. He feels the next few years will bring hypnotic regression into its own as a valid tool in psychic and psychological counseling.

"Now, for some reason hypnosis can't be used on everybody, and maybe only two out of ten people can actually have a regression experience to a past life. With the techniques we've got now, it is my feeling that as we go into the next twenty or thirty years, there are going to be breakthroughs in different techniques to enable us to go into past lives, to go into that memory bank or that soul bank or that universal bank and bring this information out. We don't always know how to use the information we get. The researchers and the people who are interested in readings and hypnosis, as these things are being more accepted, will find new techniques, new ways to improve the findings. Maybe even through chemicals, I'm not sure. At one time, practitioners were using LSD, and then, as you know, LSD became unpopular as a scientific tool because of its misuse."

In certain instances it seems that even hearing of someone else's reincarnational experiences can accomplish a therapeutic effect. Brad Steiger told me that a single case study which he and hypnotherapist Loring G. Williams published in their book *Other Lives* (Hawthorn, 1969) brought them innumerable letters and telephone calls from men and women who testified that their reading this case had helped them conquer their own fears of death. I am hereby quoting the case, slightly abridged, with Brad's permission:

> Mary Tobbin proved to be an excellent hypnotic subject. She went into light trance quickly and easily. After Bill had planted the suggestion that her skin rash would disappear, he brought Mary back to full consciousness and obtained her consent to place her into a deep trance state so that he might attempt to regress her. Mary readily granted permission, and the following transcription is a result of that initial session.
>
> *Oh, oh, I see some rats! Yeah, all sorts of rats!*
> Where are they?

*They're on a ship.*
Are you on the ship?
*Yeah.*
Where is this ship going?
*It's suppose' to go to America.*
Where does this ship come from?
*England.*
What's your name?
*Abigail Daws.*
How old are you?
*I'm fourteen.*
What year is this?
*1692.*
Who is with you on this ship? Your mother and your father?
*No, I'm by myself. I'm a servant.*
Whose servant?
*I don't know.*
How do you know who to work for if you don't know them?
*I'm going to find out.*
Oh, I see. [Abigail appears to have been an indentured servant.] Well, were you sold to someone in America?
*Yeah, I lost my money and they put me in jail.*
I'm going to count to three and we'll go back two months when you were still in England. One, two, three! Now what are you doing, Abigail?
*I'm in jail.*
Why?
*I stoled some bread.*
Do you have a mother and father?
*No, they're dead.*
How long have they been dead?
*About five years.*
How long are they going to keep you there?
*I don't know, maybe forever.*
Well, I'll count to three, and we'll take you to the day that

they're going to let you out of there. One, two, three! Now what's going on?

*They tell me I'm going away, that I'm going to America. I don't want to go there!*

Who's telling you all this?

*A big man. I don't know who he is. He's nasty. He's got black hair and a black beard, and he smells awful!*

We'll count to three and you will be on the other side of the water; you will be in America. One, two, three. Now what do you see?

*Getting off the ship. It's coming into Virginia.*

What port in Virginia?

*I don't know! I never heard of it.*

(Abigail begins to cough violently.)

I'll count to three and your cough will stop. One, two, three. What was the matter?

*I have a bad cough.*

Where did you get that, on the ship?

*No, I had it before. I don't feel very well.*

Does it make you spit up blood?

*Yes, sometimes.*

You say the ship is just coming into town? Okay, it will be one week later, so you can be settled. Now what do you see?

*I'm working in the kitchen.*

Whose kitchen?

*The Jacksons'.*

What town is it in Virginia?

*Richmond.*

How did you get to Richmond from the boat?

*In a cart.*

How long did that take?

*About a day.*

Do you remember the town where the boats stop?

*No. I was sick.*

How do you feel now?

*Not very well. They don't make me work very hard, those people.*

They're pretty good to you?

*Yes.*

What kind of a place do they have?

*A big place, real nice. They have lots of land.* (Another fit of coughing)

We'll count to three and the coughing will stop. One, two, three. What do they raise on this farm?

*Oh, some vegetables and chickens, and they have some cotton.*

Do they have a lot of help?

*They have the nigras, they're called.* [Black slaves were first brought to Virginia—and the Colonies—in 1619. After 1690 large numbers of slaves were brought to the plantations to fill the demand for cheap labor.]

But you're white?

*Yeah.*

What do you do—cook, wash dishes, or what?

*I bake bread. You take some flour, the flour they grind down . . . and you knead it . . . Then you let it set: you let it set overnight. Then you knead it . . . and . . . put it into little things.*

How many loaves do you have to make a day?

*Oh, maybe fourteen or maybe thirteen, lots and lots of them. Then you put it into the oven. It's a great big thing.*

*What is it made of?*

*Bricks, lots of bricks.*

How do you heat it?

*With wood.*

Who does the cooking?

*The black mammy.*

Do you get good food?

*Yes, pretty good. Onions, carrots, a lot of beans.*

Do you get lots of it?

*No, there's too many of us.*

What do you have for meat?

*Salt pork. Ech! I hate that!*

We'll count to three, and it will be five years later, and you will tell me what's going on. One, two, three. Now what do you see?

*Nothing.* [The death experience has taken place.]

What are you doing?

*Floating.*

All right. I'll count to three again, and we'll go back to your last day as Abigail. One, two, three.

(Violent spasms of coughing)

Abigail, you don't have to cough. I'll count to three and your coughing will stop. One, two, three.

*I'm sick. I'm in the work house.*

Where are the Jacksons?

*They're gone away. They're always gone away.*

How old are you now?

*I must be about seventeen.*

How long have you been here?

*It must be three years. It's nice and peaceful here, and the sun shines.*

Do you like it better than England?

*Yes, I'm glad I came over here.*

How do you feel? How has this cough of yours been?

*I'm awful sick. I keep coughing and coughing, and I keep spitting up blood. I'm dying, and people tell me I'm dying.*

Are you glad you're dying?

*No, I don't want to die!* (Becoming hysterical) *No, I'm too young to die! I don't want to die, no!*

I'll count to three and it will be all over with. One, two, three. Now what do you see?

*Nothing.* [The tone of the voice is now relaxed, almost to the point of total indifference.]

Where are you?

*Floating.*

Can you see your body there?

*Yep. It's lying there. On the bed. The black mammy's cleaning me up. She's lifting me into a pretty dress.*

Now what's going on?

*People are walking by.*
Do they have you in a box or anything?
*Yeah. A pine one.*
Do they have a preacher or anyone for you?
*Yeah.*
What does he have to say?
*He just says I'm nice. Yeah, I was a good girl. Then they throw me in the grave. They cover me over.*
What are you doing, just floating and watching all this?
*Yeah.*
Are you glad now that you died?
*Yeah, I like it! I like to float!*
You're going to float on a little more, a little more, nearer today now. What do you see?
*I don't know, just things. There's a field near a beach. There's lots of people.*
What's your name?
*I don't know. I don't have a name.*
Are you still floating?
*No, I'm there! I'm watching!*
We'll go on to three years later. One, two, three! Now what do you see?
*I see a house. It's just a little house. It's cute.*
What's your name?
*Mar-r-y.* (Drawing out the name in little girl fashion)
How old are you?
*Two!*
We're going back to your first day as Mary. You can tell me all about that. Now what do you see?
*Black.*
I see. What are you doing?
*Nothing.*
Where are you?
*I don't know.*
In just a few minutes now you will have to see something.

One, two, three. Now what do you see?

*White.*

Where are you?

*I don't know. Oh, look at the people! Oh, a lady there!*

What's she got on?

*White.*

What do you have on?

*Nothing. I'm about two minutes old!*

Do you remember being born?

*Nope. All those people are happy. Ha-ha! Ha-ha!* (Begins to laugh wildly)

I'll count to three now, and it will be the next day. One, two, three. What do you have on today?

A pink nightie, I like it. (Then, changing her mind) *My hands are tied in, though; I don't like that.*

I'm going to count to three, and it will be six months later. One, two, three. Now what do you see?

*I'm with my daddy. I've never seen him before. He's my daddy, though.* [Mary Tobbin's father had been in military service at the time of her birth and was unable to see his child until she was six months old.] *I'm on my daddy's lap, and they're taking pictures of me.*

Is that fun?

*No, I don't like that. I cry. I've got a pretty white dress on. Yeah, it's got green, white and red things on it. It has white and green things down like this, and great big green buttons, and white and green things around it like this. It's cute. I like it. My hair is curly.*

In his own regressions, my late friend Peter learned a basic fact: One most often remembers facts in one's life that are in some way associated with deep emotion. This is why you will recall the day you first met your wife or where you were when

Kennedy was shot, but not what you had for lunch two weeks ago.

So it is that recalling a past life most often brings forth an emotion-fraught experience. In discussing the matter with metaphysically minded men and women who claim to remember past lives, Peter also learned that reincarnational recall very often *begins* with a vivid memory of the death experience.

This also poses a problem: Your main memories may be of death, love, disappointment to the extent that more "rational" data are blotted out. So to get anywhere, you must first defuse the emotion, getting around those peaks of intensity that block the view of any one life as a whole. As a conscientious hypnotist, Peter was very careful to guide his subjects through these distressful periods with extreme caution.

"The subconscious," Alice Lane explains "is filled with a conglomeration of various emotional energies unreleased from past times in other dimensions of time and space. The other night at one of my lectures, a lady asked, 'Why is it painful when the energy is being released?'

"The answer is, of course, that at the time the incident was suppressed within the subconscious it was conditioned with a particular emotion. It is this emotion that needs to be released in order to alleviate attracting to oneself similar future conditions. Once the energy is released, one's life totally changes for the better."

"The unconscious," Dr. Leichtman explains, "is a department of the human mind that is filled with potentials, tendencies, patterns of behavior, and urges which have been accumulated from previous lives. As each individual matures, the unconscious also begins to receive repressed material as an input from the conscious experiences of the new personality.

"The unconscious does not contain the details of past life experiences; that is a matter which is only recoverable in full from the level of the immortal essence, or soul if you will. This is a matter rarely accessible to incarnate people, but unconscious elements *are* accessible—at least indirectly in most cases. The indirect access is a matter of careful observation of individual tendencies, likes, dislikes, fears, desires, frustrations, patterns of behavior, general attitudes, convictions, and so forth," says Dr. Leichtman.

Is there then a clue here, as Dr. Leichtman surmises, as to how past lives manifest their influence on current incarnations? As he points out, people do not necessarily know that they were killed in a plane crash in a past life; they just know they do not like planes in this incarnation, although they cannot trace this dislike to anything in their childhood. There is no rational explanation for it. It is, according to Dr. Leichtman, a *general* conditioning caused by past-life experiences, rather than a concrete memory from the distant past.

He adds: "The implication here is that the personality of each subsequent incarnation may be new, but there is a deeper, or inner, aspect to human consciousness that is very ancient. In psychological terms, this aspect is the realm of the unconscious. This is not the unconscious of Freud, but more the personal unconscious of Jung, who emphasized the positive and archetypal qualities that come into personal expression through the unconscious."

Whether or not the subject is actually recalling a past life, in a sense the hypnotic regression experience, is a mini-exorcism, in which the hypnotist provides a framework wherein the phobic demon might be observed from a less painful perspective and thereby be banished forever. If the hypnotist is a loving, considerate individual, he may cautiously lead his student through a cleansing of inhibiting and crippling emotions.

However, I feel it is necessary to add a word of warning concerning hypnotism and hypnotists in general. While there are many well-trained and highly qualified hypnotists throughout the world, hypnosis is a relatively simple technique. There are many who enter the field strictly for profit, with little concern for the welfare of their subjects. To them it is strictly fun and games, and their ethics are not always as desirable as they might be.

Jane Roberts' comments concerning reincarnational therapy:

"I find that people are fascinated by the subject of reincarnation, but I always suggest concentration in the *present* rather than a search for identity through a past life. I am always appalled by the people who have visited some psychic and been given a reading of a recent past life. That, to me, is really outlandish.

"I recall one case in particular. A man, a lawyer, had gone to a hypnotist and was told that he had been hypnotized once before, 25 centuries earlier, by a bad spirit who made him give up his will. The man wanted me to contact that spirit and make it release him. He really believed that story. So I simply said, 'Look, kid, that was 25 centuries ago. That person is dead now. Use your common sense. What reason do you have in this life to be so gullible?' "

While it is reasonably established that a person will not perform an act under hypnosis that is completely contrary to his conscious level of morality, it must also be understood that under hypnosis one may perform certain acts which he could resist doing in his conscious state. A simple admonishment here is: know the hypnotist before you submit to his techniques. Be certain that he is working at a true level of moral research, and not simply attempting to bring others under his mental control. Beware of the quick-buck artist with little or no respect for the individual's emotions, morals, or sanity. Certainly, hypnosis should never be undertaken as a parlor game performed by anyone without proper training and ethics. Just as you choose your doctor, dentist, lawyer, or plumber on the recommendation of others who have found his work satisfactory, do the same with a hypnotist who is going to tamper with your inner realms of being. *Caveat emptor!*

We must also consider some of the dangers involved in using hypnotism as a simple game. Remember, in hypnosis you are working with the most valuable part of your physical anatomy, your brain, and with the most treasured possession, your mind—perhaps the soul itself.

Dr. Shealy says:

"I believe that people should not get hung up on reincarnation. I have to admit that I have been a little bit guilty of teaching this technique to a number of my friends, who go around doing it as a party game. This is all right when people are well-adjusted, but if someone is seriously distressed, you could get into serious trouble.

"My mother, for instance, insisted upon listening to a tape she had heard me talk about, and I said, 'You're not ready for that!' She didn't believe in reincarnation, but we let her listen to it. When it was finished she was hysterical for 45 minutes! Not because of *what* she 'saw' but because of the fact that she had seen *anything!* It was such a shock to her to try to accept the whole concept of reincarnation that she became extremely distressed after having a very simple vision of herself.

"The only other person that I had problems with was an alcoholic for whom I played this tape. She came close to cracking up during this, because she saw herself for what she was. She did not wish to come to grips with herself. She just said pointedly that she was not ready to confront the problem.

"I do encourage past-life recall as a tool. If one has moderate or serious emotional hangups, this is a good way to come to grips with them. But there are some real risks involved with this kind of thing. It should be done by a trained person. I think if the individual has an intense interest in it, he should go to someone who is capable of guiding him through an experience without letting him crack up doing it."

Phyllis Huffman is an enthusiastic and vibrant personality, mother of three teenagers, and a public relations executive for the State of Idaho. She and her husband Jack founded a local metaphysical group that has attracted nationwide attention over the past years.

Although Phyllis has studied in the metaphysical field for a number of years, she did not gain depth in her understanding of reincarnation until she was placed under hypnosis and regressed to a lifetime in ancient Egypt. Information received seemed to tie in with many of her present-life associations and to give her life more direction and purpose at the pragmatic level. Reasons behind events of this incarnation became meaningful, and she gained understanding that could not have been possible for her without the background gained through extensive foundation in esoteric matters.

"I have noticed that people who have not acquired a good, solid metaphysical background quite often become very upset by the experience of being regressed to former lives. For many of them it is literally a nightmare, a very destructive, negative experience. They go into it expecting a lark, and instead they totally meet themselves in a naked, bare, open manner that they cannot cope with. They are not prepared to face themselves as they really are, and it opens up all types of psychological problems.

"I have found that now I am very selective of whom I regress, and for that matter have all but given up hypnotic regressions for this reason. I feel that some people simply have no business being regressed until they are properly trained in metaphysics so they can understand themselves under hypnosis.

"Many well-trained hypnotists are really doing more harm

than good because they do not properly screen their subjects beforehand. I find this extremely upsetting. We need more qualified people in the field, not only trained in hypnotic techniques, but people who are spiritually oriented and who have a good sense of personal identity themselves.

"Regressions, if handled correctly by qualified people who know what they are doing, can answer so many questions and help people in so many ways. I cannot describe how rewarding the experience can be under the right conditions."

I believe Phyllis has a valid and important point here; of course, hypnosis is not for everyone, and no one should jump into an induced trance state without a considerable amount of metaphysical understanding. I doubt that simple stage hypnosis performed by a qualified hypnotist has ever really harmed anyone. But when we are delving into the far reaches of *self*, there must be certain preparations taken to avoid psychological boomerangs. Still, knowledge of one's past lives can most assuredly aid in a better understanding of the present incarnation, and such information can answer certain psychological problems which I doubt can be answered in any other way. While hypnosis may not be the total answer for certain individuals, it does serve as a valid means of probing an area of the mind that cannot normally be reached in the fully conscious state.

Phyllis tells the results of a regression she conducted on a young man some time ago:

"A young man, in his twenties, well-built but feminine in his appearance and mannerisms, who had been reared in a very staunch Mormon home and was still living at home with Mom and Dad, had become homosexual, serving as the 'female' partner in his relationships.

"Regressions previously done by a well-known hypnotist did reveal that he had been female in past lives, and that he had carried these emotions forward into this life. While I feel that citing too many examples of the actual information acquired through regression would be an invasion of this young man's privacy, I can say that the hypnosis and information gleaned from those regressions have made him more aware of himself, and have accounted for his feminine and homosexual tendencies. As a result he is today much more masculine in appearance and manner. He has given up his homosexual practices and has much better control over his life. He now has a positive outlook on life which he did not have before. He has more self-confidence, and is more vibrant and healthy than when I first met him in 1973."

I believe that we can say the experience Phyllis related served a practical purpose in the life of the young man, who learned of his true identity and who applied this information to his present situation.

Dr. Denys Kelsey, a prominent British psychiatrist and member of the Royal College of Physicians, along with his wife Joan Grant, a woman gifted with extrasensory talents and the author of several books on psychic matters, co-authored *Many Lifetimes*. In this book they approached the subject of hypnotic regression and the possibility that such past incarnations do indeed play an important role in one's present life.

Dr. Kelsey is often asked whether every patient who is able to reach a deep state of hypnosis can be regressed to an earlier lifetime. He points out that in the majority of patients, with whom he has used hypnosis, the need to explore an earlier lifetime did not arise. Among those for whom he thought a previous personality might be relevant, only a small proportion were able to recall a single episode. Kelsey further points out that even when a patient is intellectually convinced of the concept of reincarnation and only seeks empirical evidence of personal continuity, he is not always able to help the patient gain this evidence.

Kelsey does show a case of psychoanalysis which did, to all appearances, produce a regression to a former lifetime. A tall, wirey, athletic young man, suffering from the idea that there was something feminine about the shape of his hips, had a feeling of inferiority and guilt so intense that he had been unable to concentrate on training for a career. He was ill at ease with both men and women. Dr. Kelsey found him a good hypnotic subject and was satisfied that during the course of long analysis he did not overlook any factor of his present life that might have been the origin of his symptoms. The young man was helped to the extent that he was able to derive considerable enjoyment from social activities and to complete the training for his profession. Dr. Kelsey says, however, that he had failed to solve this man's essential problem.

After the analysis was discontinued, the young man came to visit Dr. Kelsey perhaps once a year, but always on a social rather than a professional basis. Some time had passed since Dr. Kelsey had last seen the man when he received a letter asking for an appointment as his symptoms were again bothering him severely.

During the hypnotic sessions that followed, Dr. Kelsey's wife, Joan Grant, helped in the analysis. Dr. Kelsey induced hypnosis and told the young patient to let his mind wander in search of the origin of the feelings. Kelsey stressed that he would have no hesitation in expressing anything, though it might seem improbable or even bizarre.

Within a very few minutes, the patient began to describe scenes in which an elegant young woman appeared, always with a handsome escort. The scenes changed abruptly. One time the young lady would be swathed in white ermine at the Savoy and then, with no thread of continuity, she would be on the deck of a yacht or perhaps at the paddock at Ascot.

At this point Joan Grant handed her husband a note saying this was a genuine recall, but the young man was not seeing the girl as she really was, but rather the girl's daydreams of the woman she longed to be. The note suggested Dr. Kelsey should tell the hypnotized patient to see the girl herself—as she really was.

The subject quickly identified with the girl and at this point began to use the present tense. As the story unfolded, he became very distressed. The girl had been the daughter of a small tradesman in a university town and had fallen in love with a titled undergraduate. The regression further indicated that the young lady believed the man intended to marry her. She had fantasies of the life she would lead as his wife, a role for which she tried to equip herself by pouring over fashion magazines and society papers.

But when she told him that she might be pregnant, her lover was too scared to even be sympathetic and said he never wished to see her again. In an effort to produce an abortion, the young lady took excessively hot baths and began jumping from a five-foot wall, but none of these devices had the desired effect. She even began wearing a strong corset in order to prevent the swelling abdomen from betraying her condition to her parents. At the end of five months, in desperation, she sought an abortionist.

Grisley details of an operation followed. The abortion was performed in the kitchen of a squalid little house. The abortionist was an old woman who apparently panicked and fled in search of help when she realized that something had gone wrong. The girl died, still strapped down to the table, listening to her blood dripping on the stone floor, as she became increasingly colder—increasingly terrified.

The regression showed the circumstances of this death, in which the young lady found herself alone and in fear. It caused an element of her personality to become split off and frozen in the timeless present of that former life. She apparently reincarnated two years later, but this time she took a male body. Had the body been female, according to Dr. Kelsey, it might have suffered from an irrational fear of childbirth, or from phantom pregnancies. However, having reincarnated into a male body, the young man had feelings that there was something feminine, something shameful about the shape of his hips.

Dr. Kelsey later asked his wife how she had recognized the early part of the regression as fantasies of the young lady. She explained that the clue was in the fact that they were static and contained no action. Joan Grant recognized them as fantasies that the girl was able only to visualize, not what she would actually *do* in such situations, as they were outside her social experience.

Dr. Kelsey comments that had he followed the thread of fantasies that were presented during the hypno-regression he might have unraveled the patient's problem much sooner. He could not do so, however, as it led him beyond the limits of a single lifetime, which then circumscribed his approach to psychiatry. When he no longer tried to fit the relevant material into the limited framework of the patient's symptoms, with the help of his wife, the problem was cured in a single session. Dr. Kelsey points out that the word "cured" was justified, for the patient had no recurrence of the symptoms during the next eight years, and had become very happily married.

Indeed there are risks with hypno-regression when performed by an ill-trained individual, especially where the subject is not mentally stable. But in the competent hands of a trained operator, the results can prove most beneficial. For that matter, hypnosis can often serve as a springboard to the development of other psychic abilities, allowing the subject to develop his own methods of reaching into the unknown past through self-hypnosis, and ultimately to develop his own meditative techniques for reaching inner awareness. The records are full of people who have been hypnotized once and then began a rapid development of their own psychic abilities,

even to a point of becoming teachers and developed professional psychics. It is simply a matter of awakening the dormant
giant that lies within each of us. While few of us may be
*psychics*, we all have psychic potential, and hypnosis has an
impressive track record of uncovering these hidden treasures.

Nevertheless, hypnosis is but one of many tools to be used,
and probably best serves its purpose with the individual who is
not yet metaphysically oriented in methods of meditation,
dream interpretation, or other levels of altered states of
consciousness. The hypnotist, like any other helper along the
way, can only help that individual to help *himself* in searching
for the answers to hidden problems or latent abilities which
may have lain dormant for centuries.

# Chapter 10

## Dreams...
## The Link
## To Past Lives

While there are various methods of gaining knowledge about one's past lives, including hypnotic regression and meditation, it has been found that the dream state is for many a source of abundant information. The dream state can, once you learn the key, serve as a valuable aid in not only your spiritual progress but your *material* progress.

I asked Henry Rucker what he would advise the average person to do to find out about his past life and to start a program designed to benefit from such a reading.

"Well, in the first place, I would rather have a person not told what he was in a past life. I would feel that a person should first get as much information and facts about reincarnation as possible, so that he can establish within some reasonable credibility in his own mind that reincarnation is, in fact, a principle, rather than just something that was 's'posed.' If one should like to recall a past life, a few suggestions just before they go to sleep will cause him to dream about it, almost invariably. This type of recall will be a little bit more reassuring than having a psychic reader tell him that he was this or that. It would help particularly in a case where one had problems and hidden fears.

"When people are afraid of things, they should talk to their subconscious and say, 'tell me all about it; explain it to me; let me dream about it.' "

Could it be, then, that dreams have a more pragmatic meaning than we once thought?

It is possible to relive past lives while asleep. There is no set pattern to follow in order to dream of a past life. Quite often the spontaneous dream is actually more revealing than the one we had planned. The important thing is to remember your dreams of a past life, and the only way you can do this is to keep a note pad next to your bed. Immediately upon awakening, write down the entire revelation while it is fresh in your mind.

Many dreams will be evidential and literal when received, but others will be loaded with symbols. Dreams so often are symbolic, for the subconscious relates in subjective pattern, and one must learn to interpret his or her own particular set of symbols. In my book *Dream Your Way to Happiness and Awareness* (Warner Paperback, 1975) I show various ways to interpret dream symbols. I stress the point that the so-called "universal" symbols should be avoided in favor of determining your own cosmology, based in large part on what certain objects, numbers, and other symbols mean to you during your conscious state. Vital information is often transmitted in the dream state, and it is of utmost importance that you find the meaning in order to benefit from those messages. No one else can have your dreams; they are strictly your property, a well of knowledge that no one else can possibly give you.

This same key may have to apply to those dreams that reveal information from past lives. It is logical that if you have certain symbols in your conscious state of awareness, and these transmit themselves via the dream state, this same phenomenon perhaps occurred during past lives, when you may have had a different set of symbols. The information you reap from your dreams, while you are mentally and emotionally in that past life, will often come through symbolically, since they relate to events of that lifetime, and must be translated or decoded in order for you to fully understand the meaning of the dream.

Can we find meaning that is not always cloaked in mysterious symbolism, but the actual recreation of events long passed? In the case of past-life regression, we often find that dreams are quite literal and need no interpretation. They are, in reality, memories, and appear in the realm of sleep in the same manner that a childhood memory might present itself.

It is not uncommon for one to dream that he is dressed in Colonial American attire. Or perhaps he sees himself dressed in a military uniform completely unknown to today's armies. Though these dreams may be the result of having recently read a book concerning that particular period of history, there is also the possibility that *you were there*—that these "dreams" are in reality flashbacks to periods in one's own spiritual evolution.

Betty Keen is a member of Spiritual Frontiers Fellowship in Davenport, Iowa, and perhaps her dream will show how she was able to find a pragmatic direction that helped overcome a serious problem of hers:

"I was having business difficulties with fellow employees

when I experienced a dream that I know definitely to have been depicting another lifetime. I was the wife of an Oriental official and apparently felt my husband really didn't know how to make decisions effectively. I was intent upon making them myself, telling him how to function better. (I didn't like myself in that dream at all!) The dream showed my female figure in that lifetime hanging nude by the heels. Two Orientals, stripped to the waist, each with a slender rope in his hands with a fine fishhook-like prong at the end, were beating me with these hooks, tearing my flesh. When I awoke I realized that this propensity I have for telling others how to do things was a carryover from another lifetime . . . and that it was time I stopped. It made a very deep impression on me! I was, of course, able to 'take from it' and effectively apply it.

"I've always feared sharp knives. Before this dream I couldn't determine what prompted my fear—I've never been threatened by anyone with a knife, never suffered a cut or experienced any accident with a knife. But one evening when I was almost asleep a series of pictures of another lifetime 'flitted' across my vision. I was blonde, young, dressed in a long, flowing white gown, my hands tied, literally being pulled behind a man on horseback. We were in the desert, and I was walking on sand and kept stumbling. The man was angry with me, becoming more so each time I fell. When I fell once more, he gave an order, and another man drew a sword . . . and off went my head! Of course, relating my fear of knives in this lifetime to that experience enables me to better understand this apprehensiveness!"

Dee Stoltenberg, another member of Spiritual Frontiers Fellowship, recalled for me one of her own dreams: "Listening to Betty relate her fear of knives and her dream brought to mind my extreme fear of fire to the point where I don't care to use matches myself but call on my husband Larry to light the candle or whatever. It also brought to mind a vivid dream I had years ago of being an elderly woman in bed with fire all around me! I do hope it's retrocognitive and not precognitive!"

"Search within" is a universal admonishment given by numerous religious and philosophical teachers, and dreams are an excellent way for you to do just that.

But dreams, like other altered states of consciousness, in addition to probing the inner self, can allow wholly subjective thoughts to rise from the unconscious levels of one's being. There *are* vital messages to be transmitted via the unconscious state of sleep, and although possible past-life regressions must not be overlooked, a high percentage of dreams are simply the subconscious regurgitating unwanted information.

I recall a very vivid dream several years ago in which I saw a French airman of the World War I era jump from his crippled plane and plummet to the ground with a sickening thud. That dream remained with me for some time, and instead of fading, as many dreams do, it actually became stronger as time passed. I do not say this was conclusive evidence of a past-life regression in which I witnessed such an event, but it does tie in with other dreams, meditations, and past-life recalls that I have had over the years that seem to indicate that I was a flyer in that war. This may have been just one more horror that I witnessed at that time. Unless you truly *feel* these revelations, they have little value to you, and they can quite often represent nothing more than hallucination or wishful thinking. However, once you learn to feel these truths firsthand, through your own personal probing, they take on real meaning and value.

Obviously one can discount my dreams of medieval times by saying that these were simply fantasies drawing upon the material I read on that era. They could certainly be right. Later in meditation it was revealed to me that although I did have an incarnation in the late twelfth century, I was not a knight, but lived in a castle as a monk—a scribe, to be exact. Of course the dreams in turn could have influenced the information that later came through in meditation. I will not argue that point, but I will say that at some inner level of awareness I feel that the dreams and meditative information did have more meaning than simple fantasy.

Since this writing deals with the pragmatic value of reincarnation, it is logical to ask what *value* I place on these dreams and meditation that tell me that I lived as a monk-scribe.

Probably the work that I have been involved in for nearly three decades is the result of errors of commission from that lifetime when I was responsible for many interpolations of Scripture, a time when I took great delight in changing the jots and titles of the Sacred Books. This is not the first time I have been a scribe, but this time around I am trying to set the record straight in order to offset those fallacies I helped to create nearly eight hundred years ago.

Actually that inner feeling is sometimes all we have to go on when dealing in subjective matters. But you should always ask yourself what these past lives account for. What did you do wrong, or right, that can help you today, *right now*, in this lifetime? What pitfalls can you avoid or what good deeds can you enlarge upon that will make this time around more meaningful?

Joyce Messick, in addition to being the mother of three active youngsters, is also a teacher working exclusively with underprivileged children in the Cincinnati schools. I first met her during a Spiritual Frontiers Fellowship conference in Chicago. The next time we met was in Cincinnati where she, as chairman of the local SFF group, had engaged Brad Steiger for a lecture. That evening we were sitting in her living room, visiting with her children and husband Richard, when the subject of reincarnation came up.

I told Joyce I was planning a book on the subject, that would show the practical aspects of this principle. She commented then that she might be able to supply me with her own regression to a life that taught her the necessity for forgiving others the wrongs they had commited against her.

"I was recently hospitalized with a case of acute phlebitis in my left leg, and was put on total bedrest. Because of my own inactivity, the strange hospital noises and unfamiliar surroundings, plus the schedule of the medication that I was taking, I found it impossible to sleep.

"After my second sleepless night the resident ordered a sleeping pill for me. The first one had no effect, so the night nurse gave me a second pill.

"I found myself in a trancelike state. I felt as though part of me was taking part in the scene that I was beholding while another part of me was standing by as an observer. At no time was I physically aware of either fear or pain, even though the girl that I was watching was experiencing both.

"I became aware of my own physical appearance. I was dressed in a long brown robe made of a coarse type of material, like burlap. I was much thinner and younger than I am at this point in my life, perhaps 25 or so. I 'felt' that I was married, but my husband wasn't with me. I also 'knew' that I was childless.

"I was in a large room with walls made out of huge gray blocks of stone. The floor was covered with straw or reeds which were literally crawling with mice and bugs. There were grates in the ceiling that permitted daylight to come through, and it looked as though the sun was setting. At one side was an archway that contained a metal grate or gate. I knew that it was locked. There was a stone trough with water running through it and I also knew that it served as a toilet. There were perhaps as many as fifty or sixty other women and children occupying this room with me. Several of the women had babies. I also knew that my own clothes had been taken away and that I had been given this robe to wear.

"There was a commotion and a group of about twenty men

came through the gate. They were rough, bestial, dirty, and unshaven. I remember that they seemed to be dressed in leather skirts and tops that looked like T-shirts. I don't think that I could do justice to the horrible scene that followed. I saw babies yanked from their mothers and smashed against the wall. Women and children were beaten and abused. Some, like myself, were raped over and over again. It was like a scene one reads about the Nazis and what occurred in prison camps. In my own case either I was beaten senseless or my head hit the floor and I was unconscious for a while. I remember coming to and seeing the sun shining through the grate in the ceiling.

"The survivors were herded out into an arena. I remember that the sky seemed white. It was such bright sunlight. The sand in the arena was just as white. I could dimly see the people around and could hear them shouting. The circle seemed to be very large and there were people standing in groups all over. I remember standing there but not seeming to be a part of it.

"Some men brought dogs on a chain; they looked like a cross between Doberman pinschers and Great Danes. The dogs were very mean and started chasing people and tearing them apart, bit by bit. They chased one man up to the wall of the arena and tore him to pieces as he tried to climb up.

Next some other men came out, dressed in leather skirts, wearing large metal hats that covered their faces. They carried large tablecloth-sized nets made of something that looked like chain link fencing. These men fought with some of the men in the arena, but since the other men were unarmed it was one-sided. Gladiators came out armed with short swords, and they too fought some of the men who were left, but again it was very one-sided and didn't last very long. Up to this time the group of people with whom I was standing had been totally ignored.

"Behind us the great golden gates were swung open and large war chariots pulled by three horses came into the ring. They were made of metal, with great wooden wheels with spikes on them. These chariots ran the rest of us down.

"I saw myself being run over by the chariot. My left leg was almost severed from my body, and I lay in great pain and agony.

Then a soldier came from somewhere. He was dressed in a gold and silver breastplate with a short skirt made of strips of leather. The thing that I remember most was his helmet, which had a large red thing going down the back that looked like a scrub brush. I looked up in his face, and saw nothing but great love and compassion. He pulled out his sword and killed me. The thing that I remember most was knowing that the soldier was my present husband Rich.

"After this experience, I awoke in a cold sweat. The rest of the night I spent trying to decide just what had happened to me and what relationship it had to the physical problems which I was having. Out of my entire family I am the only one who has leg problems. My right leg is normal, but I have had problems with my left leg since the birth of our youngest daughter.

"I don't know if the tragic scene I witnessed truly involved me but I decided that if Karma came from unforgiveness, then I in my present incarnation would forgive all those who were involved in the horrors that she had undergone in that life. Perhaps she would have forgiven them then had she not been in such pain.

"The murder that the soldier committed was in truth an act of real love. I wonder if perhaps those who are scarred by such experiences bear the scars until they are able to forgive those who are responsible.

"Had some Karmic force brought all of us who were involved in that scene to Jewish Hospital, and were those who had been killed in the arena at this point in time and space being healed or saved by those very souls who had been responsible for their death? I don't have any answers, of course,

but I do know that for a time I shared a life and death
experience of another girl a long time ago that I won't forget as
long as I live—though I must forgive those involved."

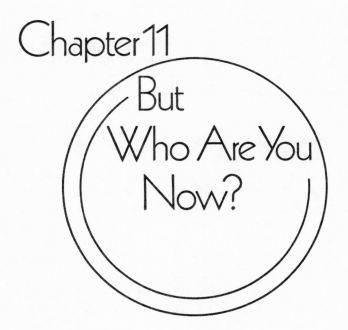

# Chapter 11

## But Who Are You Now?

One case that Dr. Shealy related to me involved a woman who came into emergency claiming she had been cleaning her husband's service revolver when it went off and shot her in the leg.

"Regression indicated that she believed she had been Anne Boleyn in a former life. As Anne, she feared her husband was going to kill her. Now I do not believe she was actually Anne Boleyn—there are many who claim to be reincarnations of famous people—but it served as an escape mechanism for her to reveal fear of her present husband and the possibility of violence from him. We do not know whether he shot her or if her story was true that she shot herself in the leg, but this type of mechanism is sometimes used. It's a little like the young man who comes into the doctor's office to talk about a disease his friend has, and the doctor says, 'Okay, let's pull your pants down and look at your friend's disease!' It becomes a way to put the responsibility elsewhere."

This case struck a particularly sensitive nerve with me, for of the hundreds of regression reports I have studied, the people claiming to be reincarnations of famous personalities, ranging from Attila the Hun to Zoroaster, are legion. In fact, at one time I truly wondered whatever happened to all the poor, simple folks from former times, for the only ones who reincarnated seemed to be celebrities. Perhaps Dr. Shealy has a valid point: that it is the "Anne Boleyn syndrome" or the "Julius Caesar syndrome" we are dealing with, people who pick up these personality traits as an escape mechanism.

Dr. Leo Louis Martello of New York City is the author of fifteen books including *Witchcraft: The Old Religion* and the controversial *How to Prevent Psychic Blackmail.* He is founder of the Witches Liberation Movement and Director of the Witches Anti-Defamation League. He edits *Witchcraft Digest* magazine and the *Wicca Newsletter.*

Often when lecturing or appearing on a TV show, Dr. Martello's sense of humor is evidenced when he is asked, "Do you believe in reincarnation?" He usually replies, "No, I don't. I once did, but that was in a past life!" Dr. Martello states:

"Past lives, future lives, other lives—the preoccupation seems to be with any life except *this* one. As a Witch I believe in the Law of Karma and Reincarnation, but I also stress that the only life which is important is the one here and now. Logically, today is the foundation of tomorrow. And today is the tomorrow that you worried about yesterday. To the extent that you make the most of this life are you assured of a better one in the next incarnation.

"What has tended to discredit reincarnation are those 'past-life freaks' who were always of the nobility, famous, or accomplished. I once attended a gathering in which there were five people claiming to have been Napoleon in their past lives, and at least three others who were Marie Antoinette! With a straight face I said that I was a stable boy in one of my past lives, which probably explains why I have to put up with so much manure in this one!

"Logic is totally absent from those who occupy the freaky fringe of the Occult. Don't they realize that by making such absurd claims of past greatness, they are only revealing what a come-down this present life is? That what they're really saying is that they are reincarnationistic has-beens? That if they were so noble or famous or accomplished, what went wrong in this incarnation? Even if remotely true—if the explanation is that this life is so lowly because of wrongdoing in a past one for which they are now paying a Karmic debt—wouldn't a sense of pride, if not shame, want them to keep it to themselves?

"The purpose of reincarnation is to make personal progress. Those who claim past greatness, but whose present life is mediocre, indicate *regression*. And even assuming that they were brought low in this life to make up for misdeeds in a past one, a Karmic debt which they have to pay, this is a *moral* issue and should in no way affect the *intellectual*. Intelligence and morality are not synonymous. There were many geniuses whose personal conduct was reprehensible, and thousands of intellectual idiots whose morality was admirable."

To feel a certain relationship to past events or eras is not abnormal in the least. However to always visualize ourselves as having played roles of greatness in the past could be a mistake. Consider that there are more people living on the Earth today than have lived throughout all recorded history! Yet how many of these people today are famous, wealthy, or even local celebrities? Most are engaged in nonglamorous fields; very few are millionaires, movie stars, or world-famous personalities. They are laborers, housewives, salesmen, business, or professional people; but few are known outside their own communities. Why, then, is it so often the case that one remembering or thinking he remembers a past life comes up with Napoleon, Ivan the Terrible, or Abraham Lincoln?

Perhaps Thomas Edison had the answer, for it was his theory that the soul is like a swarm of bees, and upon death the various particles (bees) fly away from the corpse and later become part of many personalities of later incarnations. This, of course, could account for the "Napoleon" or "Marie Antoinette" memories. If Edison was right, perhaps literally thousands of people today are composed of the spiritual fragments of personalities who achieved greatness throughout history.

I do not personally subscribe to the Edison theory, for my research over the years, coupled with personal experiences in past-life recall, indicates to me that we are complete individuals with our own personal problems to work out through a series of incarnations in which we have been a multitude of *personalities,* but always the same *individuality.*

Dr. Martello has a good point when he says: "It's fascinating to read of documented case histories that indicate someone has lived before. But the point is, how does this apply to you? What is your own personal proof, as opposed to belief? Even assuming that you lived before . . . so what? What can you do with this knowledge? How is it helping you now? If one is to achieve in this life, one must assume full responsibility for his or her own life and not use reincarnation or other beliefs as a cop-out."

There *is* a practical side to the whole principle of reincarnation. But the thing we must understand is that for the principle to be pragmatic, we as individuals must learn from the past in order to apply those lessons to today's chain of experiences so that we might make this incarnation more meaningful. If someone thinks she was Marie Antoinette, that *still* represents a "reincarnational" first step. It will do her a lot more good to start from that assumption and analyze its meaning than to dig for other, more probable lives.

Dr. Leichtman told me of a pervasive and devastating problem case referred to him by another doctor. This patient was currently hospitalized for acute and chronic alcoholism. There were also complications—considerable confusion of the schizophrenic type, which involved "rather remarkable and capricious changes of behavior and identity," raising the question of overt possession by harmful spirits. Dr. Leichtman related:

"My role in this case was to investigate the matter psychically to determine what was going on inside her mind. Was it truly a case of possession, or was it a breakdown of her personality with the negative content (id forces) of the unconscious taking over control of the conscious mind? This is a matter that is best determined by psychic means, as it can probe the matter directly rather than presume a diagnosis by inference from indirect effects."

The information obtained about this person was rather remarkable:

"Her record of past lives had been a history of repeated difficulty and irresponsibility. In the Middle Ages there had been several lives spent in the most miserable squalor imaginable. There was very little impulse to cultivate humane traits, and the outward result was quite minimal. The personality was usually very slothful and filthy in habits. Existence was maintained mainly by begging or stealing. Internal motivation was virtually nil; the only thing that stimulated the personalities was external threats and beatings.

"In the eighteenth century she was born into a poor

laborer's household. Again she was lazy, critical, and quite uncooperative in family matters. As soon as she reached puberty, she (it was a female incarnation this time) discovered sex and began immediately to use it to attract attention and receive favors. Alcoholic sprees also began about that time.

"In a short while she was arrested for stealing and sent to prison. There she suffered rather terribly, despite offering her body to her jailers for certain privileges. She hardened her attitudes a great deal during this time and became quite aggressive, hostile, and abusive in mouth and deed."

Dr. Leichtman stated that after she was released, she returned to the same life-style of promiscuity, alcoholism and being dependent on the support of whatever male companionship she could find. Life soon became a matter of chronic confusion and an alcoholic daze. She passed on in her middle thirties of malnutrition, tuberculosis, and alcoholism.

In another incarnation, she was born as a boy, but lived only a few days because of serious congenital defects.

A short time after, she was reborn in another male body and managed to live into young adulthood. The personality was strongly rebellious and totally irresponsible, indulging in nearly constant bickering and fighting. At an early age he died after a brawl with his drinking companions.

The most recent life was in the late nineteenth century as a man once more, whose mother had been a prostitute. The father was one of several Civil War soldiers in the area at the time. The entity was very much unwanted, his mother having tried three unsuccessful abortion attempts before he was born. One week after his birth his mother abandoned him. He grew up in an orphanage of a very poor quality. The home was operated by outwardly saintly types, who in reality used the children as a substitute for slave labor and were actually quite cruel to the children.

Shortly after the age of twelve, he ran away. Work was

considered some impossible insult by this time, but within a few days he joined a labor camp of men to serve as a minor servant and cook's assistant. This was a time of his apprenticeship for gambling, drinking, cursing, cheating, and stealing. He caught on rapidly, and was caught shortly for stealing and was expelled from the labor camp.

The next few years, according to Dr. Leichtman, were spent as a vagabond with brief work here and there, occasional stealing, and much moving about. In his thirties he was caught raping a young lady, was arrested and eventually hanged.

It was one more life wasted in irresponsible action and contempt for human welfare and property.

Dr. Leichtman summarized the case thus: "Examination of her current personality revealed very little basic change in habit patterns and attitude. But this time there was a more severe breakdown of the mechanism of consciousness so that she was unable to stabilize her attention long enough to control her mood, thought, or action much of the time. There was such a lack of compassion and consideration for the rights and welfare of others that it amounted to a hole in her consciousness—and a literal hole in her aura, through which she was vulnerable to the thoughts and curses of others and malevolent spirits.

"On the basis of this analysis, I concluded that there was very little hope of significant change for her. The lack of internal resources and strengths was simply too great."

This is a situation, according to Dr. Leichtman, in which one would expect very little interest or insight on the part of the subject for a knowledge of her past lives. Reincarnation data probably could not help her, but could explain something about the evolution of a serious psychological problem. It was apparent here that this person brought with her the seeds of her own continuing difficulty with alcoholism and an inability or unwillingness to cope with life's obligations. She was born with an unconscious (mind) already filled with such negative habits and tendencies.

"Serious reflection on this matter might be helpful to those who seek to blame social conditions for personal difficulties. Responsibility, and especially the lack of it, appears to be a continuing problem," Dr. Leichtman commented.

Another point this case revealed is that there seemed to be a deterioration of consciousness that carried over from one life to another. "Most importantly, this case tends to give substance to a statement that a colleague of mine once made regarding a similar case: 'It must have taken more than one life to get that bad!' In my experience, serious psychological problems all have a record that extends into the distant past, and this record contains the roots of serious problems. For example, there was the episode of the congenitally deformed body, suggesting that the mental patterns for a healthy body were damaged. The severe confusion, possible hallucination, and hint of possession in the current life seem to be the result of severe abuse to the mind and emotions in this life and in several of the previous ones. The mental damage of both alcoholism and hateful rebelliousness seems to be cumulative." Dr. Leichtman's direct investigations into the mechanism of consciousness verifies this matter.

If reincarnation is indeed a valid hypothesis—if we have trod this earth-path many times before—the theory applies to everyone equally, regardless of the present fields of interest in which one might find himself. The housewife, salesman, truck driver, or teacher might logically find that he or she has served a similar role in one or more past lives.

Jack Dempsey, former World Heavyweight Champion, says that he is a firm believer in reincarnation, that he has lived before as a boxer, and that he will return to once again capture the boxing title. Dempsey, who is nearly eighty years old, says he believes he has always been the same basic person he is now, and that fighting seems to be his destiny. There are others who believe they have lived in past times, playing the same role they are noted for now. General George Patton often said that he knew he had been a warrior in other eras of history.

Ann Fisher told me of a young man, seventeen years old, whom she had counseled:

"I shall call him David S. from Troy, New York. He was in his last year of high school and doing very badly. His mother was quite upset with him. This was another young man rebelling against authority. Although he had fought his mother all the way about coming to my office for a consultation, he sat down and relaxed as soon as he arrived. I said, 'You want to devote your life to sports. You would like to be a great baseball player.' As I started to read him, I said, 'There are many things about Babe Ruth and yourself that are common. You will be very successful in your career, but please do get through high school.'

"I had said he was *very similar* to Babe Ruth. Later we checked it out, and we found they were both the same height, 6 feet 3 inches; their weight was about the same, 215 pounds. This boy made two home runs on July 21, 1971; and on July 21, 1921, Babe Ruth made two home runs. On this particular day Dave did not hit the ball very hard, but it went out 500 feet, which was very similar to what Babe Ruth had done. Their batting averages were similar, so I would say that he *could* be Babe Ruth reincarnated. He's seventeen years old, a very handsome, very intelligent boy, and I do feel he will go ahead in this career.

"Some people continue to come back as the same type of person. For example, I read for a young lady, Deborah M. I found that she had been an actress many times. She started out in ancient Greece as a man, and had lived about 27 lifetimes. She had been on the stage each lifetime, and in each succeeding life, since Greece, she had been female.

"When I age-regressed Deborah I found that she came back
from a very recent lifetime in the 1920's. She had been an
entertainer in a "speakeasy" during the prohibition era, hating
all of it. Her father had been involved with Chicago gangsters.
The reading was very evidential, and her life had ended when
she was murdered by the gang. Once she was exposed to this
area of her former incarnation, she could remember much.

"She also went back to the 1800's and found that she had
been Rochelle, the famed French actress. She gave us some very
valid information about a bracelet given to her by Queen
Victoria, which we researched, as well as many things about
Rochelle's life that I think proved very valuable to Deborah.
Although most people will change and do other things from
one life to another, Deborah wanted only to keep acting. She
chose to come back each time with the same profession."

In my own case, I believe that I have been engaged in
writing in the past, as well as in business ventures. Both
influences have their value in this present incarnation, for I am
not only a writer now, but I also handle the business
management of Other Dimensions, Inc.

Does this mean that we are "locked in" to play certain roles
throughout all time? Of course not, for this would hardly meet
the criterion set by most Reincarnationists, that we are here to
advance on the cosmic scale; to do so, we must have a variety of
experiences.

Ann Fisher recalls the following case:

"Jane M. from Latham, New York, came to see me, and
immediately as I tuned in to her vibration I said she had been a
famous dancer who died in 1933 due to a car accident.
Psychically, I could see a car of that vintage. I told her she was
killed due to a head injury. She was quite well known — not a
movie star but a dancer, who had a lovely voice. At that point
Jane got up and started to sing and dance in the style of the
1920's. 'You know,' she said, 'I've always been able to do this. I

always wanted to go on the stage, but my family always held me back.'

"I told her that I believed that in this current lifetime she was not destined to come back and do this, as she had chosen something else. I said I thought she should know this. I told her that I picked up that she died in March 1933, and then asked her what year she was born into this life; she replied, 'I was born in October of 1935.'

"I commented that she had rested for only two and a half years before she came back, and I asked her if she now had headaches that she could not account for. She said, yes, for years she had had pains in her head, and no doctor was ever able to discover what caused them. I told her these are from head injuries in the past life.

"She then asked, 'Well, Ann, who was I?'

"The only thing I could come up with was a big initial *M*. I told her to please go and research it, so that she might find out who she was. The practical aspect of her rearing came to the fore: when I saw her about a year later, she told me that she was so glad she had had the consultation with me, because she had lost her desire to go on the stage and she could give her full effect to her present career."

But can one not follow the same basic careers and still gain that wide range of experience? There are many living today who are engaged in music, who feel they have been engaged in that same field in the past. If we choose to believe that nature is not wasteful, this in itself may lead to a reasonable amount of logic. Consider the individual who has studied business procedures in a past life and who became a successful merchant. Would this not allow him to earn his livelihood better in this incarnation and contribute more to his community, while at the same time learning certain necessary spiritual values? I am sure the Cosmic Intelligence that rules the universe could care less how one earns his living, providing he can advance a bit in each lifetime at the spiritual level.

Each life today is in reality a volume of many biographies, each woven into the present personality of every one of us. The sooner we are able to delve deep enough to understand those past incarnations and how they affect our present life, the sooner we will be able to truly add practical dimensions to our being, giving our lives more meaning.

It was late afternoon in November, almost dusk, as I entered the office of Henry Rucker, the well-known psychic and healer in the Chicago Loop. I had been in Chicago all week, interviewing various psychics on the subject of reincarnation, but I had not been able to get together with Henry earlier, as he had been out of town.

It was good to see my friend again. We exchanged the usual greetings as we sat in his office where he is president of Psychic Research Foundation.

"How have you benefited from past-life recall?" I asked. "Has it made you a more aware person? Has it made you better able to help others?"

Henry replied: "It makes me more realistic; it makes me a more complete person. I began to recognize things that were not a part of this present personality. I began to recognize agencies or personalities from the past, manifesting themselves through this vehicle and expression. And it has enabled me to have greater insights into other people as well as myself. It has caused me to change my outlook on myself, a little more self-esteem, but a little less ego, if you please. So it has brought me into a sort of situation of balance."

Henry and I continued our interview and suddenly he personalized the conversation by doing a flash reading on me:

"The only way I would use reincarnation is to have a person realize that he has certain drives, certain tensions or certain fears. For example, a person may have been locked in a dungeon — *you've had this experience!* I've seen you locked in a dungeon. You may have a thing against being locked up or dislike dark places right now, in this lifetime. Don't let it bother you—it's just that you had so many years in that dark, clammy dungeon that now the thought of being closed up in any kind of place is a horror to you. You like your freedom."

Henry's spontaneous reading did clarify certain things in my own thinking. I have had a certain empathy for anyone in prison, and over the years I have corresponded with several prisoners throughout the country. As a news reporter I would shudder when the judge sentenced anyone for even a short term in jail, thinking of how this person's freedom was being taken away from him, although knowing that his crime undoubtedly justified the sentencing.

I do not like tight places, darkness, or damp surroundings, but I never really gave too much thought why. Henry managed to jog something in my long-forgotten past, however, that does make sense.

"That personality thought how wonderful it would be to be free. Now your present personality is utilizing that particular incarnation, because this one is the philosopher. In those long days of darkness you learned a lot and thought a lot."

I have always considered myself more of a journalist than a philosopher, but perhaps Henry is right in that reincarnation is a philosophy, and having spent many years researching the subject the philosopher must come out occasionally.

"As you sit there, you are composed of about ten personalities. These personalities are on the subconscious level—past lives. From time to time they work like pistons in an engine: the warrior comes up; the philosopher comes up; an old Chinese comes up; the priest comes up; the Egyptian comes up; the Atlantean comes up—*when they are needed.* We are programmed to the extent that we will manifest a given number of personalities while the present personality is growing.

"The only reason that you sit here and are able to do one thing is because of the past experiences that you've had at other times. I think the personality 'Graham' is in the training state as personality. At one time it will also be a very important factor in a series of new personalities."

If we do believe basically in the theory of rebirth, then we must also accept the idea that under certain conditions we can establish a rapport with our individual pasts which serves as a link of some practical use in our present lives.

Journalist Wanda Sue Parrott is a newspaper editor and columnist, formerly with the *Los Angeles Examiner.* She is also an author, with such credits as *Automatic Writing* (Sherbourne Press, 1974) and *Auras* Sherbourne Press, 1975). She is a contributor to several other books, including Brad Steiger's *Medicine Power* (Doubleday, 1974), and two New American Library books, *Dangers of the Psychic Jungle* and *The Bermuda Triangle* (1975). Wanda Sue is featured in the motion picture documentary, *Death Is Not the End,* a film dealing with reincarnation and precarnation possibilities under hypnosis.

"I have found, since beginning the wonderful reincarnation experiments with Elroy Schwartz and Dr. Kent Dallett of UCLA, that I am capable of performing many feats that might be explainable only through reincarnation. For example, I healed my son's crushed hand by manipulating the fragmented bones. In five minutes, the swelling, blackening, and puffy joints had returned to normal. I was able to upholster an antique chair and make it look good! I was able to whip up uncanny foods in the kitchen, purely by listening to the inner voice. Normally, I am confused by housework and confounded in the kitchen! And I am all thumbs at the piano, yet on a few occasions my hands played beautiful music.

"Was this evidence of reincarnation? Or was it a demonstration of the Biblical adage: Knock and it shall be opened unto you; ask and ye shall receive? I have discovered that if I consider my brain to be a door and my thoughts a hand that can knock on the door, saying, 'I need to know how to cook,' suddenly inspired thoughts will tell me exactly what I need to know. The only time this failed was when I petitioned for help in some plumbing. No amount of reincarnative experience or contact with cosmic intelligence helped me repair a broken fixture. Only a bona fide plumber could do the job.

"Generally, however, every practical problem of living can be solved by drawing on the available intelligence within my own mind. I believe all humans are natural born mediums. I know that I am. I further believe that intelligence is indivisible. It matters little to me whether I receive intelligent guidance from 'this side' or 'the other side' or whether or not I will ever come back to live again. What matters most is taking today and spending it well, because the very moment in time in which we are is right now."

Do not concern yourself with whether you are an "old soul" or a "young soul," for the number of past lives you have had makes little difference. The important thing is that you are here now, living an incarnation at this very moment in history, and you must make the most of it.

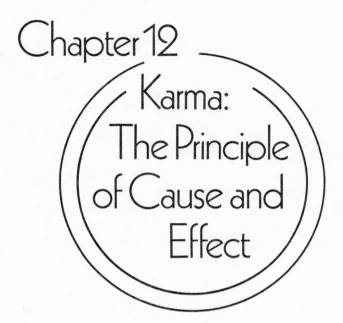

# Chapter 12

## Karma: The Principle of Cause and Effect

Actress Ann Miller, interviewed in the October 22, 1973, issue of *Midnight*, tells of her belief that she is now paying for sins she committed thousands of years ago when she was a queen of Egypt. Miss Miller began her current career as a belly dancer, before Hollywood discovered her, and has always associated with things Egyptian. She first suspected her tie to ancient Egypt when she visited the Metropolitan Museum in New York City as a child. There she found herself drawn toward the Egyptian artifacts—especially the carved statue of Queen Hatshepsut.

Several years passed, and by now Miss Miller was a motion picture star. She was in Egypt, filming on location, when she visited a psychic reader who told her that she was indeed the reincarnation of that queen of an early Egypt. The seer told her that many men would come into her life, and that several of these men would die, because in the previous life, as the queen, she had given orders for these same men to be killed.

The old woman continued by telling Miss Miller that when she ruled Egypt, she committed the sins that followed her to this day, and that while no harm would come to her, it would be her fate to lose close male friends through death. She said that one of the men would die of an incurable disease, another from a heart attack, still another would develop a stroke, and a fourth would die due to a problem related to his nose.

While Ann Miller's career skyrocketed, her personal life became something less than serene. Here attorney of some twelve years died of a heart attack. Another close friend, Charles Isaacs, died of an incurable blood disease. A doctor who had proposed marriage to her went into surgery for a minor nose operation—and died. The final prophecy came true when her husband Arthur Cameron died, following a stroke.

Is this ample evidence that Ann Miller was the Egyptian queen now reaping the harvest of Karmic debt, or is it pure coincidence that the Egyptian seer's predictions came true?

According to Ann Fisher:

"Karma is a Sanskrit word meaning action or reaction or simple cause-and-effect. Christians say, 'As you sow, so shall you reap' or 'do unto others as it should be done unto you!' Most Christians see the cause and effect taking place during one life, whereas Reincarnationists carry it over from one life to another. According to the Law of Karma, a person is born into many lifetimes under the exact set of circumstances with the exact endowment he would need to utilize his best qualities, which he has found and developed in previous lifetimes.

"There is an appeal to reincarnation that makes it easier for more and more people in the West to accept. The opportunity to meet fresh challenges in new lives is now received by many who would rather believe in rebirth than the old cut-and-dried theory of Heaven or Hell. It appeals to one's sense of fairness. It is a concept of evolution based on the laws of cause and effect.

"During the time between your last death and your present birth, you have chosen the situation in which you now find yourself, in order to correct past errors. You spin around in the wheels of life. You may sometimes be rich and sometimes poor, changing from time to time in sex and race. Many believers think that every possible type of existence can occur to anyone on Earth during their many incarnations.

"I feel that reincarnation answers many questions that religion has left unanswered for so many years. We may ask why people suffer so much in their lifetimes when they seem to be innocent of any apparent wrongdoings. We wonder why they are trying so hard to accomplish certain things, and cannot. The average person may feel that this is unjust; only reincarnation and Karma come up with an answer.

"The Law of Retribution extends over one's entire Karmic cycle, so that the soul may reap in one lifetime what it has sown in another. This is a comfortable theory so far as I'm concerned, because I feel orthodox religions do not offer such practical answers to problems. I feel the law of cause and effect works.

"I remember an instance when I was lecturing to the Association for the Blind. The question came up about reincarnation; I did not want to answer the question because many of them might be blind in this lifetime as retribution for putting out someone's eyes in a past lifetime. I really think that negative things do come back, just like all the good you do. If in a past life you were a great pianist, a great artist, or a great psychic, you would come back with this ability. You might not pursue that talent this time, but you would have the ability."

Ann stresses the necessity for all of us to learn to live the best possible life this time, so that we need not cover the same paths of error again. She believes that through an acceptance of the principle of reincarnation mankind may someday learn to abolish crime and war and the other evils which retard our progress.

"KARMIC DEBTS INSTANTLY DESTROYED" was the lead-in to a classified advertisement that recently appeared in a national publication. It's not that simple. No one can destroy or even alter your Karma. Karma is something that only you are able to do anything about. You would not be reading these words now if you had managed to erase all negative aspects of your Karma. What you have been in the past has determined what you are today, the circumstances of your life, the kind of parents you have, the economic conditions you were born into, as well as those you still experience at the present stage of your life.

To some, reincarnation is a logical cop-out by which they can blame their present bad habits on patterns formed in ages past. They may take the attitude that one can eat, drink, and be merry, for the next lifetime is soon enough to correct their flaws. This attitude, of course, is not limited to those professing a belief in reincarnation, for many have felt they could raise a little hell in their youth and "get religion" when they were too old to do anything else.

Both, sadly enough, are wrong, and they misinterpret the entire meaning behind the principle of rebirth. Of course you can overcome Karmic debts, and you can benefit from Karmic accomplishments of past lives—in fact it is necessary that you do so—but no one else, for a few dollars, can release you from *anything* your individual soul has built up over the course of past lives. Others may help you realize what those debts and virtues may be, and they might offer suggestions that can help you along life's present path. But do not join the gullible who try to pay their way out of Karmic responsibility, for in the long run you may find yourself building even more negative Karma for failing to recognize its universal meaning and to do something about it yourself. True, if you keep erring this time, you most assuredly will be back, for there are certain lessons to learn and problems to solve, but the cosmic clock doesn't tick for you alone. If it takes a dozen lifetimes to learn one simple lesson, so be it!

The events of today are fleeting, and the old adage that nothing is as old as yesterday's newspaper holds true, but it must be remembered that what we do today will definitely affect what we can expect to be or do at some future time. That future may be years beyond the grave, for this current life is the place where we set our future Karmic patterns. Metaphysicians state uniformly that our main goal in life—including all past and future lives—is to gain perfection or At-One-Ment with the Creative Force or God. The admonishment, "Ye must be perfect, even as your Heavenly Father is perfect," is the equivalent of this sentiment in Christian metaphysics. Similar admonishments have been made in most religions and philosophies.

Unity School of Christianity, Science of Mind, and numerous other metaphysical schools and churches throughout the world believe in reincarnation, but they spend very little time teaching its concepts to their parishioners and students. They feel the key to spiritual progress lies not in concerning oneself with past lives, but in gaining as much perfection as humanly possible in this one; this may be another possible reason the doctrine of reincarnation was dropped by the early Christian Church.

Several years ago I went to Lee's Summit, Missouri, and

Unity Village. It was a beautiful weekend, and my wife and I decided to take off, as we often do, for a short trip. I had not written ahead for reservations, and when we arrived we found that this particular weekend was practically a blank on the school calendar. Classes were not in session, and most of the key people were away for a holiday. It may have been a blessing in disguise, for we were not committed to a rigid schedule, but were free to roam the grounds, relax, and just visit casually with those still on campus. There were no conducted tours, just a handful of people walking around, meditating in the chapel, and in general enjoying the tranquility of Unity Village.

After dinner one evening I became engaged in a conversation with a Unity minister. Since I was researching material for my book *Eternal Journey*, I asked him why Unity did not stress the reincarnation principle more. I knew from years of Unity study that reincarnation was a basic tenet of the philosophy, but not an active part of the teaching.

"Well, Mr. Graham, let me put it this way," he began.

"While we do acknowledge the idea that we have all lived before, we are really more concerned with the idea that each student must learn to make this life count as much as possible. While we acknowledge that complete perfection might be impossible for most in a single lifetime, we at least want them to strive toward as much spiritual gain as possible, now."

In my interview with Evelyn Paglini, a Chicago psychic counselor, I mentioned that people so often use Karma as an excuse for their behavior, saying in essence: "That's my Karma. That's why I am such a bad person." Karma is so often thought of as a negative thing. Need this be the case? Miss Paglini replied:

"Many people use it as a crutch or as a scapegoat. No, Karma need not be bad. You are not always paying for something you have done in past life. You may be an 'old soul' who is attempting to build its character, build its strength, in order to advance into a different dimension, a different cycle. In doing so, you will take on specific tasks that will strengthen yourself. You may take on a deformity, or you may take on an accident, possibly in early youth. This will cause you to be dependent on another individual. It will teach you humility; it will teach you understanding; it will teach you how to cope with other people, who have chosen to be placed where you are the burden on them.

"In essence what you are doing is building yourself, because you have the temptation there to become sarcastic, irritable, and to wallow in self-pity. But being able to rise above it, being able to realize that this is the strength of purpose you have been looking for, you will be able to say, 'I can still be useful, I can still give of myself, I can still benefit, I can still utilize my mind,' instead of becoming a vegetable and taking out your spite on the world. Take the experience and make it positive, and grow from it.

"It's a question about which you can go into such depths and such lengths that you could fill an entire book with the answers. There are so many different aspects to Karma and the reasoning behind it."

I asked Henry Rucker if he believed that we are today the result of what we were in past lifetimes.

"Yes and no." Most concepts of reincarnation state that our problems today are the result of something we did, bad or good, in another life.

"Now I take the position that bad or good is only a reflection of how you feel about life. To one person, smoking is horrible; to another person it is a relief, it is therapeutic, and a whole lot of other things. So we can't take a thing and say it is bad or good. Life is not bad or good, life *just is.*

"I think reincarnation is exemplary of the idea that life is a continual thing. Now that is the first thing that we learn—and eventually humanity will learn in this New Age—that life is a continual thing. The fact that we reincarnate is incidental.

"In other words, here's God, a billion years old. How could we possibly be able to understand Him in the brief span of 70 to 100 years? And I say that our experience of God cannot be on a vicarious level, it has to be a *real thing*. The only way that you can know God is through a series of experiences. So with God, I think, as with destiny, we have to use various vehicles to get the variety of experiences that there are to know and understand what you are in terms of God.

"I don't think that reincarnation involves retribution and reward as much as most people think. I think that the experiences that you had as that other personality would not determine any punishment. If you were born crippled, I would think that this experience manifested to teach a soul that it could survive under the most adverse conditions, rather than because you had thrown some Christian to the lions.

"I don't attribute all of the experiences that we have had to something that we did or did not do in our past lives. I think we're moving beyond the concepts of heaven and hell and our next step is to get out of punitive and rewarding Karma. We are guaranteed safe-conduct through this experience by God. No matter what happens to you, it is not necessarily the result of something you did; Graham never did anything to anybody because he's just a short time around."

Wanda Sue Parrott only hints at specifics concerning the pragmatic role that rebirth may have served in her life, but her views of the continuity of life should be shared with others:

"For people like me—down-to-earth skeptics who have also glimpsed the heavenly regions of light and color and all-pervading intelligence reincarnation is a word that needs redefinition. Perhaps the term 'continuing cosmic con-sciousness' would be a better term. I believe it is the spirit, not the flesh, that constitutes the real personality. And until we can give the spirit a mortal name, and identify it scientifically, and prove that certain portions of the infinite essence spill down over and over into life forms, as the Vital Life Force, we will continue to speculate on whether man will live again.

"I ask the question: has man's spirit ever died? For persons fearful of death, reincarnation can offer a respite from terror. For those afraid their souls will be punished in hell, reincarnation offers a chance to make up their weaknesses and right their wrongs and thus avoid the insufferable."

Joe De Louise commented:

"I feel Karma's all *good.* I feel that it's like a person committing a crime and going to jail for a couple of months or a couple of years: he should feel that he has paid back society, or paid his debt to the Universal Law. It should free that person to go on, to grow spiritually. I say that Karma is good, because when you accept the fact that you're serving out a Karma, it can get rid of a particular problem and permit you to move into other areas, growing and spiritual areas.

"Show me or tell me one thing in Karma that could be good or bad. In other words, what could be bad? If a person abused his stomach by drinking heavily in a past life and comes back with a very, very sensitive stomach, he may constantly have stomach problems; that is a built-in rejection of the alcohol, the device that will prevent him from wrecking another life. In other words, it makes a person more sensitive. So you can't say, 'I've got a bad Karma, I came here and I can't drink!' It's a *good* Karma. It serves its purpose."

Father Nathan of the Foundation Church of the Millennium in Chicago says:

"To say, 'That's my Karma' is fine, but Karma is personal responsibility. This means we have created a situation for ourselves, the situation that we currently are facing. To say 'That's my Karma' is alluding to some outside force, when in fact the Karma is something we have created.

"The point is that it can be a hangup word, a cop-out. If it is your Karma, then it puts you in a position of control with respect to it. It's instructive. All Karma is good and all Karma is bad. It's bad in that it binds us (what Karma literally means is 'bonds') and keeps us at a particular place. We sow our seeds, tie our knots, and involve ourselves on a particular level of existence. As long as we are producing Karma, as long as we are creating Karmic effects, we are bound to that level of existence, so in that sense it's bad.

"But in the other sense, as we approach our Karma head-on, it gives us insight into what we have been, what we are, the effects we have created. It allows us to undo, or rather it provides within itself the means of undoing it.

"Man's basic dignity is the responsibility of being able to face one's Karma and dealing with it—to accept, this is me, this is what I have done, this is what I have been—all this, good, bad, and indifferent, is me. It's not 'them' out there; it's not external forces. This is something I have created, I have made, I have put upon myself. Only in seeing it that way do we give ourselves the power to change the situation. We put ourselves in absolute power with respect to the things we want to achieve,

"I feel that Karma gives important perspective. Without it, things don't make sense, in terms of my cosmology. However, to get overly obsessed with Karma is as distracting and illusory as to ignore it. It's a perspective; it's a point of view; it gives you a relevant reality; and in so doing, it allows things from the past to be brought into time, to be resolved, to be dealt with, to be discharged. But a constant attention on the past is as irrelevant as no awareness of it at all.

"You have to be in the present, and very often what happens is that someone has an experience that relates to some past life, and he feels fascinated with something that perhaps has a romantic flavor. He then builds up an entire illusion of his present life with respect to a past-life memory. We are what we are; we are born; we are mentally reborn; we are born of the parents who are allowed to us. We are born into the situation that influences us. We go to schools that are right for us, right in terms of what we need to do in this lifetime. This is where it's at for us right now.

"Whether we like it or not, the point is that we are responsible, and that's where we should keep our attention. The past is relevant insofar as it gives us insight into the current situation."

Eursula Royce feels:

"We may have flashbacks to those eras of time we would like to be in. Perhaps these are created experiences, or experiences of something that we need to know to relate to this lifetime. But I don't feel that it has anything to do with a fixed pattern of life. If so, we would have to do away with the theory of cause and effect. We would have to do away with the theory that we make our own happiness or unhappiness. We'd have to do away with natural laws which have been passed on through the ages, and we would have to do away with the theory that meditation will elevate us. We would have to do away with all those theories, because no matter what one believes in, if he believes that he has a Karmic debt to pay, he has created a negative aspect that will obstruct his attaining his goals in life.

"I feel that we do need negative responses in our life to help us grow, to help us understand life. All of life is not positive. We would not be here in a learning process to elevate or evolve if we did not have something to relate to. If we never had the experience of seeing someone ill or being ill ourselves, or having a financial disaster at one time in our lives, we would not be able to understand others' problems. We have quickly to learn that we have to apply ourselves to all kinds of responses to get anything out of life.

"I feel everything in life is good, whether it be negative or positive. I believe that every negative has a positive response; it is a process of learning for us."

Henry Rucker aptly summed up the idea of Karmic relativity when he said:

"The sun coming up for some guy who's going to be electrocuted today is a bad scene. For a guy who's going to get out of jail tomorrow morning, the sun can't come up fast enough. But the sun still comes up. It's the same sun, and it isn't bad or it isn't good."

Arlene Grant and her husband Dan were taking one of their usual weekend trips to escape the rat race of the big city. Since they both enjoyed nature, they decided to head toward northeast Iowa with its rolling hills, woods, and trout streams. Suddenly, as they approached an intersection, Arlene turned pale with fright and began to perspire across the upper lip.

"There was a fire here! I can see a cabin burning, and people burning alive!" she told her husband. "It's horrible!"

Within a few minutes Arlene regained her composure: she said that it was a weird experience and that she could not really account for it.

Nothing more was thought of the incident until a few weeks later when they were once again heading for these "North Woods." As they approached the same area, Arlene once again said she felt as though she were burning up. This time, however, she added that she saw Indians arguing with a frontiersman before they set the cabin afire.

"Now, that doesn't make sense," Dan commented. "With the exception of the Spirit Lake Massacre, Iowa had few problems with the Indians."

Dan is a radio and TV journalist in a large city in Eastern Iowa, and he had occasion one day to do some research that took him to the local library. There, in a small volume published primarily for the edification of the citizens of Fayette County, he ran across the report of a little-known incident called the "Teagarden Massacre," involving a frontiersman, his family and two Indians.

It seems that a T. Gardner had supplemented his income from farming his few acres by selling whiskey to the Indians. On one occasion one of his customers had left a rifle in lieu of payment for the "firewater," with the understanding that he would return in two weeks with the cash.

The two weeks passed, and in keeping with the tradition of honesty, the Indian did return with the money. But, T. Gardner, in keeping with the tradition of greed, had sold the rifle.

A heated argument ensued. The enraged Indian left, but returned later that night with a friend, and the argument continued. Finally, after much drinking, one Indian struck Gardner with a piece of furniture, knocking him unconscious.

It was not clear whether a lamp was tipped over or if one of the Indians deliberately set fire to the cabin, but after they left, two of the children, a boy and a girl, reportedly escaped to a neighbor's cabin about a mile away. The wife had not been at home during this time, but after the embers cooled and neighbors were able to check through the ashes, the body of T. Gardner and another younger daughter were found.

Dan and Arlene avoided this intersection on future trips north, but Arlene was not satisfied. She knew she had scored a "hit" on the psychic level, having known of the fire long before her husband stumbled across it in the limited-circulation history book. But what connection, if any, did she have with that fire?

About four years later, the Grants attended a lecture in southern Illinois, where they happened to strike up a friendship with a professional hypnotist. During the course of conversation, the story of the burned cabin came up, and Arlene expressed her belief that she might have been the young girl who had escaped with her brother that night. The whole scene was too vivid to release as pure coincidence.

"Have you ever been regressed?" asked their new friend.

"No," was Arlene's answer. "I doubt if I would be a good subject for hypnosis."

The hypnotist offered to give it a try, if she was willing, as the story seemed to hold some fascination for him.

She was a good subject, excellent in fact, and she was into a trance within minutes, as Dan and others watched the regression in their motel room. The hypnotist gave a pre-hypnotic suggestion that Arlene would at all times be aware of what was taking place and of what she was saying, but that the hypnotic state would be deeper than the reverie state.

After regressing Arlene to the day of her birth in this current incarnation, he said, "Now, we shall go back in time to a former life that holds a practical meaning in this current life."

At this point Dan thought to himself, what practical value can a life as a pioneer child hold to this one? In spite of the earlier strong feelings about the burning cabin, Arlene has no undue fear of fire in this life, and certainly no uncomfortable feeling about Indians, having been reared near an Indian settlement early in this lifetime. Perhaps, he thought, the regression will go to some far-distant past life.

"What year is it?" asked the hypnotist?

Arlene, as the previous personality, that of a three-year-old child, thought, but could not visualize, a date. (What three-year-old today is aware of such matters?)

Again the question was asked, and she blurted out, "1880."

"No tie-in here," thought Dan, as the Teagarden Massacre was much earlier, 1847. Then he realized that probably the last date registered with Arlene in her conscious state was 1880! They had been to a railroad museum that same afternoon, and the plate on a woodburning locomotive read "1880."

The hypnotist was satisfied, however, and proceeded with his questioning. "We are now going to go to the last day of your life. It is now just a few minutes before your death. You will feel no pain—no emotions—you will be viewing everything as a witness, *but you will not feel pain!*"

"They are arguing."

"Who is arguing?"

"My father and two Indians."

"Where are you?"

"Under a bed."

"What are they arguing about?"

"I don't know, but they are very angry."

"It is a few minutes later. What is happening now?"

"One of the Indians is picking up a gun. He hits my father in the face with it. Now they [the Indians] are leaving. My father is unconscious. There is fire all around."

"What happened next?" asked the hypnotist.

"I don't know. We must have burned in the fire, but I seem to be just floating around now."

"Where were your mother and sister and brother?"

"Mother wasn't there at all. My sister and brother were hiding under another bed, but left right after the Indians left. I don't think they knew I was under the other bed."

The hypnotist then gave Arlene the command to rest for a while and told her she would hear nothing being said until he commanded her to hear his voice again. At this point he turned to Dan, to verify dates and other data concerning the Teagarden Massacre.

Dan confirmed most points except the date, 1880. He also pointed out that Arlene had always had the feeling she was the girl who escaped with her brother that fateful night, not the younger daughter who perished in the blaze.

The hypnotist then continued the regression, this time

attempting to find the essence of that young life that had bearing on this current incarnation as Arlene.

"Now, I want to search in that life, and tell me what lesson you may have learned. What mistakes did you make that you feel need correcting now?"

This question puzzled Dan a bit, for his reaction was that a child so young could hardly commit a great error of any kind. However the answer was soon offered.

"A toy!"

"What kind of toy?"

"A doll."

"What about the doll?"

"I broke it, and then hid it, so I would not be punished."

"Why do you feel you would have been punished? Children often break toys."

"I stole it from another girl. I was afraid I would be punished for that."

"Was there a lesson here?"

"Yes, I knew I must never steal anything again."

This, of course, could be the pattern that was set for this life, for after reviewing the tape of the regression, Arlene (now fully conscious) commented that her present-life father had always been very strict on such matters as honesty, often admonishing his large family to never steal anything.

"I'll vouch for that," Dan added. "She won't even get something out of a girlfriend's purse when asked to do so, but will bring the purse itself to the friend. That honesty seems to be a thing with her." With a chuckle, he added, "She doesn't even pull the traditional wife trick of going through my pockets for change at night."

Dan commented to me later that the only point he was worried about was that the regression was after the fact. He had researched the Teagarden Massacre as it is recorded in the small history book, prior to the regression, and had discussed this with Arlene. However, he was rather impressed with the idea that while she had always thought she had escaped the blaze, the regression indicated that she was the young girl who had perished in the flames.

He also pointed out that Arlene is always cold in this life, wearing sweaters and jackets when the temperature dictates light clothing in the hot and humid Iowa summers. He, being rather hot-blooded, literally roasts in the 80+ degree temperature she requires in their home during the winter months. If she was the young girl who died in the super-heat of a blazing cabin, that tragic act may have set up certain psychic patterns which now require more than normal heat to maintain body comfort for Arlene.

As for the lesson to be worked out in this life—that of not stealing—that could be fact, for honesty is one of the virtues required of the evolving soul. Although the child was quite young when she stole the doll, and later destroyed it to hide her guilt, the lesson may have been dramatic enough to cause a trauma that had to be later erased from the Karmic debt of that entity.

In some respects this regression may seem trivial, but remember that in the theme of events concerned with reincarnation and the atonement of Karmic debts, we are often dealing with minor events in the purification of the individual entity. Not all of us were Hitlers who have to erase the sin of killing six million human beings in the ovens of concentration camps, but deviation from perfection must be overcome if we are truly to "be perfect even as your Heavenly Father is perfect."

The more you familiarize yourself with the past, the better you will become equipped to deal with the present in order to make this incarnation more meaningful and effective, as well as to avoid the pitfalls that could boomerang in some future incarnation.

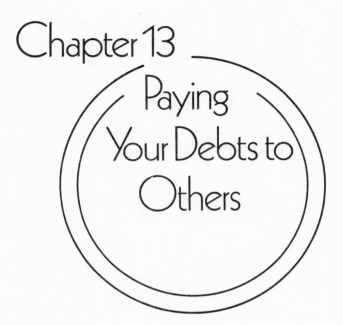

# Chapter 13
## Paying Your Debts to Others

I do not believe that *you* choose the personality when you come into a new body," Henry Rucker says. "I think this is something that is arranged by God, or the Lords of Karma, or whatever you want to call God. I think the experiences that you have, that you are to acquire, that you need, are the various personalities that have been selected out of the vast number that you have had, but only ten will be utilized in any incarnation.

"Now, if you start an experience maybe twenty lifetimes ago

and, because it was so brief, you continue that experience again, you are naturally reborn near the people who started the experience with you. The relationships that you would have with those people would vary. For example, you might be with a person now to whom you would be very hostile, or you might be with one for whom you had a tremendous amount of love."

This seems to make sense. Several lives have been revealed to me in the altered states of consciousness of meditation and the Alpha stage regressions: one as a Roman businessman, another as a Monk, and a couple that date to widely separated periods of Egyptian history. But the one that seems to serve its key position in this present time is the World War I incarnation, where I built up a Karmic debt with my longtime friend and spritual brother, Brad Steiger. If I "remember" him easily, it's probably because we have a good deal to work out with each other.

If we accept the basic theory of reincarnational/Karmic linkage to others, and agree that we are drawn together with our contemporaries from past lives for the completion of Karmic patterns or repayment of Karmic debts, then we must eventually meet these entities in the flesh. In that case, the recognition should be mutual—but is it always?

"When you do meet an 'old' friend," Matt, my editor friend from New York pointed out to me, you *can* often find him 'irritatingly familiar.' But the clues are often a lot subtler: a sense of disquiet, of being unfairly pigeonholed into a new role. Once when I was with someone who I finally sensed had some important connection, I got physical chills. I didn't feel cold, but my teeth began chattering and I actually stuttered, indicating some high excitement on a subliminal level.

"Once a girl said upon first meeting me, 'Well, well, *he's* here.' But when I met Brad, as well as this young lady, *I* didn't feel any sense of recognition."

So, before we are too critical of others' assessments of past-life recognition, perhaps we should give serious thought to the idea that they may be right. Perhaps it is we who are lacking in our inability to recognize them as part of our former incarnations.

Earlier, Brad Steiger mentioned the people who say, "Don't you remember when you were my brother during our lives in Atlantis?" or "You have changed some, but don't you remember when you were my father during the reign of Thutmose III in Egypt?" or "You were my husband in ancient Greece, but I forgive you!"

These statements ring a bell with me, too, for I have yet to lecture on the subject of reincarnation without such dialogue arising during the question-and-answer period or later when visiting with various members of the audience.

Normally I try to be diplomatic and say that I do not recall the incident but that perhaps it will come to me later. Usually it does not come to me, but it does leave me wondering if this person may be hitting at some level of truth.

I have also experienced these fleeting glimpses into the past and seem to "recognize" certain people in the audience or at gatherings around the country. I know that I do not know them from this present lifetime but know, also, that they represent some link to the past. Quite often after the talk I have the opportunity to visit with that individual and know instinctively that he or she has no similar recognition of me.

I am sure these individuals are telling the truth, but I am equally convinced that I am picking up some fragment of truth at certain levels of awareness in my recognition of others. What then, is the answer?

We have all had the experience of seeing someone who looks like someone else—mistaken identity—and within minutes we are usually able to realize that this is the case. This person just resembles another, and we think no more about it. I had such a thing happen to me several years ago. I was driving down one of the main streets in Cedar Rapids, Iowa, when I suddenly noticed a young lady standing at the bus stop. She looked for all the world like my wife. The bus stop was near our son's home, so I assumed that she had gone over there for a visit. I pulled up to the curb and started to open the door when suddenly I realized that this was a woman I had never seen before! Yet the resemblance was striking.

I told my wife of the incident that evening, and she commented that a friend had recently told her she saw her hanging out laundry a few days earlier at a house on that same street. We did not live on that street or even near it, but two people were sure they had seen my wife there, myself being one of them.

Of course we are often guilty of mistaken identity in this life, so is it unreasonable to assume that you or I may look like someone who has been in an individual's past-life recalls?

Also, as Matt points out, "It makes *great* sense that reincarnational memories tend to differ. Talk to three guests at a wedding. One will say he wept, another had a great time, the third was deeply moved. A married couple will usually tell widely differing stories of how they first met. People remember what was important to *them* , so quite naturally their recall of shared past experience will seem quite different. Recall that Brad remembered only my first name; my Dalmation port of origin had nothing to do with our day-to-day affairs."

I am sure that you have experienced this yourself. You see someone you instinctively *know* was linked to you in the past, and may sense the relationship—a brother, lover, sister, or parent or even a business partner. Yet the other person does not share this "instant recognition."

These individuals who approach public speakers and claim former acquaintances are not kooks or crackpots at all, but usually intelligent individuals trying to establish what they consider an identity with another person. I am convinced that the majority attending lectures of this type are sincere and serious in their search for answers. They are seekers after truth, the same as the rest of us. They only mean to try to establish those long-lost ties that are in their reality, whether or not the same bonds are evident in the reality of others. Who is to say whether they are right or wrong? Certainly I will not take the responsibility for accusing them of a falsehood, intentional or otherwise. For that matter, who is to say I am right or wrong in feeling a strong attraction to another individual who obviously does not also feel the strength of that bond, or at least does not openly say so. But, if the other person does not also realize the recognition, what can be gained by it? Do not drop it altogether, but give it some time to surface, and you may be pleasantly surprised to find that the other person will eventually put two and two together and come up with the same "four" you have.

"Obviously," Matt says, "the trick is to get the problem out in conscious light. But the more serious it is, the faster it bubbles up. That's why you don't *need* to play reincarnation games. If you recognize someone and they don't recognize you, that's *your* problem, not theirs. Chances are you can let it go. But if any real reincarnational drama is about to unfold, all you need do is grant it permission. It'll leap up and practically belt you over the head."

Matt is currently collaborating on a book called *Growing Up Psychic*, in which he examines the everyday social and psychological consequences of "unorthodox" experience. Here and elsewhere, I'll quote from the manuscript:

"We know of a young girl, an only child, who had a most unsteady relationship with her father. He once confessed to her that she was not *exactly* an only child, and that she had two illegitimate half brothers. For some reason, she felt proud of this. Some years later, when the two were attending a seance, she began screaming at her father for having seduced her mother several hundred year before. In *that* life, the medium told them, her father had been a happily married man with a large family, and she was his single illegitimate daughter. In this life, the roles were exactly reversed: she was the only legitimate heir to his property, and thus had a chance to be born on the right side of the blanket.

"Naturally, the medium had no knowledge of this unorthodox family history. But the girl and her father couldn't possibly say how fantastically 'right' this past life seemed—not without seriously compromising themselves.

"One reason why reincarnation still seems a disreputable topic is because the 'proofs' are so often indiscreet. Again and again, we have found that past-life Karma is perfectly, ironically mirrored in *this* life experience. The parallels are so striking as to make even a skeptic think twice. But why don't such case histories emerge in print? Simply because it's relatively easy to accept that one has been guilty of murder, adultery, or incest in the past, but it's far harder to own up to equally bizarre configurations in *this* life, of which the past is simply a mirror image.

"We've also seen cases in which past-life lovers are reunited, but both in bodies of the same sex. Even if they remain only casual friends, a past-life investigation can't help but bring up present thoughts of homosexuality. If your past 'associate' is now of the same sex, it's far easier to say I know you killed me, but I forgive you,' than 'I recall that great weekend we spent during the Saturnalia.'

"On the other hand, reincarnation does suggest that we shouldn't be too hard on ourselves, or each other, for sudden eruptions of extramarital, premarital, homosexual, or incestuous longings. If Antony and Cleopatra both came back as executive vice-presidents of an ad agency, would they be content with an occasional nod in the corridor? Yet, there are countless examples of people who give in to sexual attraction, only to find out that the affair doesn't work out. From a reincarnational point of view, we would know that sex has simply been bait to get these two back in contact. Once the sex is satiated, of course, they're again faced with whatever problems they *originally* had to face. Chastity is almost irrelevant; it's the basic syndrome of commitment, debt, and antagonism that has to be played out, and it is hoped, settled.

"Again and again, we've found that sex *by itself* is not a Karmic problem. Rather, it's the battleground on which other personal problems are worked out."

A good example of this point of view involved a young man in his early twenties who came to Dr. Leichtman requesting a past-life reading. There were several relevant lives that he related, but he found that the young man's most recent life was particularly significant.

"This was a life spent in the nineteenth century as a man. The general temperament of this incarnation was that of a rigid and hypercritical, puritanical bigot. He was a very compulsive and rather paranoid businessman who had worked very long hours and fussed over others who lived in a more leisurely manner and enjoyed themselves. Actually, he disliked most of humanity and had such a nasty disposition that no one could get along with him. So he condemned and criticized others who did have a more normal social life.

"But he also had a lusty imagination and set of fantasies about young ladies. He didn't overtly do anything about these desires, but he often committed mental rape and adultery."

According to Dr. Leichtman, the young man also managed to become involved in a very fundamentalist type of Christianity during his adult years, and he used his religion to help police his own barely restrained lusts, as well as to gain the opportunity to demonstrate his own bigoted righteousness. He was miserable, and he sought to "share the misery" by being outwardly very moral and condemning of others.

"After I related this story, the young man confessed that he now was quite the opposite. In fact, he could not immediately relate to the story at all. It seems that he was born into a very fundamentalist family this time around. His mother was especially viperous and puritanical. It also turned out that from an early age he had been struggling with strong homosexual urges. Thus far he had restrained himself, but only at a great price.

"To make matters worse, he had a rather flabby and effeminate body and mannerisms, and an unfortunate lisp. If that didn't make him obvious enough, to add to his miseries, he stated that his mother was virtually able to read his mind. The implication was that if he ever really went out and did something 'wrong,' she would know immediately without his telling her.

"Whether the item of his mother's alleged telepathic ability was true or not, this was certainly a miserable and guilt-ridden young man, and the case demonstrates how unpleasant tendencies to criticize are met with the consequences of suffering from a narrow and bigoted lifestyle and mother. Whereas he had previously hidden his lust and overtly condemned others who exhibited even minor degrees of it, he now no longer could hide his passions or act them out. Where he callously amused himself with illusions of superiority and purity, he now suffered from massive guilt and inferiority feelings."

Dr. Leichtman is not sure how much justice this man saw in his current personality traits and proclivities being the consequence of previous indiscretions, but he hoped that in time he would. Hopefully, this explanation would give him a sense of meaning again about his suffering, as well as pointing the way to resolving his current conflict. Dr. Leichtman told the young man that he needed to learn tolerance of human weakness in others and to gracefully accept his own weaknesses without so much self-condemnation. It was not sex, but rather the life-strangling rigidity and narrow puritanical ethic of his present religion that he had to examine.

In another case—that of a lady in her thirties—we see a different set of sex-related problems. She had been reared by an extremely neurotic mother who later had to be periodically hospitalized for mental illness. Her childhood was barren of love and filled with fear and frustration.

Later on in life she drifted into a marriage which she found dull. Although she worked part time, the only excitement she found was in occasional affairs with men. Between amours she consumed herself with a great deal of thought about romance and glamour. A major part of her time was involved in planning meetings with her lovers and in reviewing and fighting about the relationships. Life was one great tragic mystery to her. Fate had dealt her a low blow, and she thought she deserved a little happiness.

"In her past lives, she had an overt, long-standing tendency toward selfishness and irresponsible action." Dr. Leichtman commented. "In her immediately previous life, she had been a rather vain and frivolous woman who was insanely jealous of her older sister and her boy friends. She had treated her mother with great contempt and rebellion."

As Dr. Leichtman reported, by her late teens in this previous incarnation she was going after men with a cold and calculating heart. She was determined to find the most glamourous and dashing men so as to flaunt her success on all of her competitors. As it was, she ended up marrying a clever con man who had only his good looks and pretentions as assets.

She quickly cultivated contempt for her new husband, and continued to look elsewhere for a fulfillment of her romantic illusions. There was a great deal of secretive activity during the rest of her life, but it was more foolishness being acted out than the cultivation of mature relationships. Her affairs were shallow, colored with soap opera glamour.

"During the whole of that life she never gave much thought to anything or anyone of value in her life. Romantic illusions and fantasies commanded her attention and, of course, produced nothing worthwhile. Her great vanity and selfishness repelled both the people and the experiences that might have eventually brought her fulfillment and happiness.

"Her current life was a general repetition of the previous one. This time she drew a mother who was incapable of giving love and attention. As she had only contempt for her previous mother, she was now to endure a horrible experience designed to help her appreciate the value of having a good mother who cared and approved of her.

"And again, the same inability to recognize and appreciate things of value plagued her. She could not fully appreciate her marriage or position in life, and she sought to bring romantic fantasies to life once more. Not having the discernment to seek out someone of value, these affairs were also unhappy.

"This time around, with insight and assistance, she is learning to recognize the elements of fault and distorted attitude and desire in her. Slowly, there is a considerable correction of error and a growing maturity in her.

"Here is another case in which environment cannot be blamed for her current disposition and lifestyle. The seeds of her own discontent were born with her, as the unredeemed tendencies to ignore responsibility and to run after some pleasant illusion."

Nancy French related the following to me:

"The Quasar television advertisement, 'works in a drawer,' describes Karma beautifully." Karma is 'works in a drawer' — previous works! If each person could be his own repairman 'on the outside,' he could change the central nervous system circuitry, give the cells something else to remember.

"As I was traveling along a highway, I noticed three women standing alongside their car. I had passed the car, when I heard a telepathic 'Help!' from the soul of one of the three. I sensed the urgency so I turned around and drove back to the scene. By that time a policeman had joined them. The gasoline tank had ruptured, and gas had spilled onto the pavement. Very impressed with the feeling of something imminently disas-trous, I brought my attention to the immediate surroundings to see the policeman standing at the edge of the spilled gasoline next to one of the young women who had a lit cigarette in her hand. 'Don't drop the cigarette into the gasoline.' I cautioned. She threw the cigarette a distance away from the danger.

"There were verbal and telepathic thank you's all around and a tremendous feeling of relief. The woman—the soul owning the present-time body—had 'asked' for help to change a pattern of death by fire! If it had been photographically possible to take a picture of what occurred on an energy level, it would have shown a black cloud of danger that simply dissipated when I said, 'Don't drop the cigarette into the gasoline.' The policeman commented, 'I'm terribly afraid of fire!' Yes, he was because he had been with the young woman in other lifetimes when she had burned to death!

"Reincarnation and incidents from other lifetimes control subtle levels of consciousness, so there's no freedom in most instances because the electric circuitry remembers and puts out the same recording.

"The quickest, easiest, most stable way of ridding one of what he doesn't want from another body lifetime is to *get some new wanted problems.* A problem, as I define it, is something one wants to do, something one wants to be, something one wants to have—goals. When one gets about the business of being, doing, having goals, or entering new arenas, he is giving the cells *something new to remember.* The law of displacement—putting something desirable in the place of something undesirable—cancels the negative; one doesn't have to worry about ridding oneself of the undesirable if he is doing the desirable. That's *practical reincarnation.*"

Forgiveness is the key to breaking the Karmic debt structure. We help others by forgiving them the wrongs they have committed against us in the past. We in turn are allowed to overcome our Karmic debts when those we have wronged forgive us. Often we balance the scale through new experiences which sometimes take on the form of our undergoing the exact treatment that we have shown others in past lives. What simpler way is there to prevent future Karmic build-up than by making those corrections now?

# Chapter 14

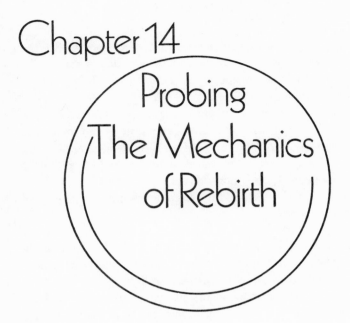

## Probing
## The Mechanics
## of Rebirth

Gavon and Yvonne Frost point out: "Modern Christian dogma is being replaced with new belief in reincarnation based on the Hindu ethic of the lawgiver, Manu. However, to many philosophers this transmigration, or degenerate form of reincarnation, has many flaws. If you are 'bad,' says transmigration, you will be punished by coming back as some loathsome beast; so you must *ipso facto* be 'good.' Further, transmigration implies that you must endure any present misfortune passively, because at some time in the past you were evil and your present misfortune is the natural evening-up of the score. In the Akashic Record, your name is on a page of debits and credits which must in some unspecified way be balanced if you are to get off the Wheel.

"But these theories of transmigration and resurrection do not seem to fit in with what has been learned from regression techniques nor with concepts of an afterlife as described by Ruth Montgomery's communications with Bishop James Pike, nor yet with the famous Myers experiments."

Instead, the Frosts hold the Wicca philosophy of progressive reincarnation:

"Let us consider the idea that a spirit comes from some unspecified source and inhabits an Earth plane (or planet plane) shell so that it may learn and grow.

"A spirit came from a pool of what we like to call Divine Fire, inhabited the first elementary creature, and gave it life. By inhabiting this living body, the spirit grew; then in returning to the pool of Divine Fire, it caused the pool to expand as well. Thus as the Cosmos and the living beings therein grew and expanded, so the controlling Divine Fire also expanded, keeping pace with the needs of the Cosmos. This pool of energy has been called the 'fifth dimension' or 'eternity' by a British mathematical team headed by Professor Bennett, who finally formulated a United Field Theory—something which Einstein worked toward during his entire life. As the Cosmos expands, it loses energy, since theoretical physics requires that the energy level be constant. Only by formulating the Energy-Pool theory were the mathematicians able to explain a structured Cosmos.

"As the Cosmos expanded and life became more complex, the Divine Fire correspondingly expanded to keep everything in balance. We see here an illustration of the idea attributed to Hermes Trismegistus: 'As above, so below.' For as we get levels of development on the planet plane, so levels of spirit development occur on the other side of the Invisible Barrier, a place which is often called "heaven" but which we simply call Side.

"The *raison d'être* for our existence, then, is a growth system: As the Cosmos grows, so do our spirits. And the total amount of energy stored in the pool also grows. This has often been called the 'boarding-school hypothesis.' The spirit inhabiting the lowest level of any given animal species, perhaps *Homo sapiens,* has come from a less complex being. Thus we can detect in some levels of mankind animalistic, anti-social behavioral patterns.

"The being on the Earth plane learns, grows, and dies. That spirit then progresses through a short time at home in Side to another more complex assignment in a suitable body. This assignment can be likened to a further learning experience at boarding school. The progress shown here is upward, as the spirit grows and learns to handle assignments of ever-increasing complexity. The time the spirit spends at home—in Side— serves to assimilate and synthesize new knowledge and (in conjunction with guide spirits) to select the spirit's next school and assignment.

"Let us for a moment speculate on one set of criteria: selflessness versus competitive behavior. Consider an assortment of your acquaintances. Can you separate them into, say, four or five groups which are progressively less competitive, ranging from those who love violence, roughhousing, and blood sports, to those selfless individuals who refuse to compete? Which group would you place highest on your personal ladder of progression? The selfless ones? If a life of total selflessness is a means to avoid reincarnating again as a human, though, might it not actually be selfish to live a selfless life?

"It is important to recognize that many thinkers do not

place human beings at the top of the ladder of progession. For if social behavior or intelligence is to be the criterion of spiritual development, dolphins are far more advanced than mankind. Many philosophers have attempted to decide what criteria should be used to define development at the human level. Apart from a definition of nine levels on the Earth plane (and congruently—as above, so below—nine levels in Side), our tradition is silent on these criteria.

"Remember that in a modern Unified Field Theory, the energy which may be 'spirit' must increase as the universe expands so that cosmic energy is kept constant. But the system is also reversible: when the Cosmos starts to contract, spirit energy will necessarily have to diminish. So the reincarnation cycle will then flow backward, approaching zero at the ultimate single-nucleus cosmic state."

I asked Eursula Royce if she felt we are today the result of our past lives:

"I feel that we were born to become what we are today. I believe that we're very carefully taught by the time we are six or seven or eight as to our concepts and our beliefs in life. We are taught by our parents or whoever teaches us those concepts, until we reach an age of understanding; then we're able to pick and choose our own truths and beliefs. I feel that we learn, through trial and error, through cause and effect, quickly, which way to go in life. We are living in a world where we meet many vibrations; we touch many lives; and we're going to pick up many things from many people.

"Two human beings come together to plant a seed for a child, and they are part of its life and part of others' lives.

"Sometimes we fall into very heavy categories: We could ask the question, why does one child die at the age of two, while another person lives to be 65 years of age? I do believe that if there is an energy called God, that we have to undergo certain changes in our life that we have to experience. When a child dies, it might be as a result of some kind of a learning process the parents have to go through.

"I do believe that spirits attach themselves to individuals, and they attach themselves very strongly from the time we are born. We're given what, in a lot of belief systems, are called 'guardian angels.' When we are ready to evolve, they are there to help us advance. They don't tell us what to do or what not to do, unless there's danger or something very negative in our life. Then they're there to help us through it. But when we're ready to accept the spiritual side of life, I believe that they're there to give us some kind of a truth they have learned, that they are working out so that they can evolve on that side."

"I would say that reincarnation is a truth that is found probably on an individual level, in an individual mind, and is understood when a person evolves to that point of understanding where he can accept it. I think when we talk of reincarnation, we're looking for something that's way out, when actually it's really very simple."

The American Indians basically believe in life after death, and also in obtaining help from those who have passed into the spirit world. Many Amerindians also have a strong belief in reincarnation and accept it as part of their Medicine, their spiritual way of going.

Twylah Nitsch is the granddaughter of Moses Shongo, the last great Seneca medicine man. She lives today with her husband Bob in her ancestral home, which was built on the Cattaraugus Reservation in Upper New York state well over one hundred years ago.

Twylah, the Repositor of Seneca Wisdom, has agreed to share her views concerning Seneca thoughts on reincarnation:

"The teaching of my people in viewing reincarnation involves a great range of beliefs, in that its beginning is linked to former lives through evolution. I can only offer my experience in this life and show how reincarnation through evolution has influenced my daily existence. I am aware of my former lives, or forms of evolution, because they are the source of my spiritual and material seeking. My clan is the Wolf. It is preceded by the Deer. The lessons of these creatures has created instincts and manifestations in this life. The manifestations appear as characteristics of wolves and deer lifestyles. The source of personal comfort stems from the animal instincts and is the point of beginning that makes me begin my search. Therefore, in each succeeding lifestyle, I carry knowledge crystalized from former lives. For deeper understanding I have focused upon this animal level, because we all carry animal instincts. There would be no growth without the framework of former lives to support the present life. That little statement was often heard in this family and is said to have been a cliché of the people of Wisdom and the Medicine people. Here is the lesson of former lives and future lives, as it was presented to me."

1. You have been born into this material environment to be guided by this family and Nature's Universal Family.

2. Your talents and abilities thus far have been developed during many previous life experiences, to prepare you for this and future life lessons.

3. Your teachers are from the spiritual levels of more advanced evolutions, as well as some from the limited physical environments. This means also that the teachers are not necessarily human beings, but come from all walks in Nature's environment.

4. There is cumulative knowledge of former lives building the foundation upon which this and future life experiences unfold. This knowledge is the source for drawing the power to grapple with these lessons on your chosen path of enlightenment.

How has this philosophy been meaningful in my life? I shall answer in the same idiom:

One, I am aware of my spiritual and material environment and what it has to offer by giving me purpose through direction and action.

Two, I do not travel alone because I am part of the holistic concept in universal communication, learning, understanding, developing, practicing, and sharing.

My gratification and happiness is number three, and it lies in knowing that my spirit goes on living in many bodies, and that this life is measured by my depth of environmental awareness, spiritually and materially.

My goal is number four, to share my knowledge with others as revelations of spiritual enlightenment. If I may help others awaken positive direction, they can nurture self-understanding and reap an abundance of health, material enrichment, benevolence, and peace of mind. Material enrichment in this case can be defined as walking in balance under spiritual guidance.

As a psychic medium, Ann Fisher says she has been trying to find evidence either to support reincarnation or to prove it fraudulent:

"I'm open, but during my many years as a psychic consultant I have found there is more proof that reincarnation is a reality.

"I have found one idea very, very evidential: that poeple who die when they are very young—before their early twenties—come back quickly, because they somehow feel they didn't complete their former life. Many times a person will come to see me, and will say, 'I've had such a fear of death; I feared I was going to die at 19. But I didn't die; why didn't I?' This person may be 25, and I will say to him that he is remembering a past life in which he died at 19, but came back fast, in order to pick up those years that were lost in that lifetime.

"There have been numerous cases where I have been able to trace past lives of people who came back in a very few years. Other people may have had very fulfilling lifetimes, and wish to grow on the other side. They may not come back for a hundred or two hundred years. Some do not want to come back at all.

"For example, Ann S. from Troy, New York, came to see me

one day, and asked why she could not receive the spirit of her mother. 'My mother has been dead for seven years, and I have a feeling she has reincarnated,' she said. She asked whether it is possible to pick up an entity that has reincarnated, and I told her, no. If the entity has found another body, I would not be able to pick her up, to give her communication.

"I was not able to get anything about her mother in our first sitting, but about a week later Ann's brother Bill came to see me. He is a police sergeant from another city in New York.

"After one point in his reading I picked up his mother's past, and I said, 'Your mother died seven years ago, but six months later she reincarnated. She wanted to come back fast, and she was born in India where she is now six and a half years old. Her name is Elizabeth, the last name is Indian, a name I do not get, but she is half English and half Indian. I feel she is starving to death. I feel she chose the wrong lifetime, and this is why I have not been able to give you communication, because she is not in the spirit world.'

"About a week later Ann S. received a letter from an orphanage in India asking her to support a child. A picture of the child was enclosed, along with information about the child. The child's birthdate was six months after Ann's mother had died. Strangely enough, the child's name was Elizabeth, and she appeared to fit the detail I had described to Ann's brother Bill in the reading.

"Ann asked whether she should support the child. I said, 'Evidently you wanted to get in touch with your mother, and she has come back to you through the mail,' so I suggested she send some money and see what happens.

"About a month later she got a letter from the orphanage saying they had no such child there, but they kept the money. All I could conclude from this was that Ann had wanted to contact her mother and her mother had manifested in the letter from the orphanage in order to get the message through as to where she was.

"Later communication proved to us that her mother had died of malnutrition in India, and we were then able to pick her up, since she was back in the spirit world. In a later reading her mother said that she had made a mistake by coming back too fast, choosing the wrong lifetime, and that she suffered, but that she now wished to stay in the spirit world and not be reborn. This seemed to satisfy Ann S., for she felt now that her mother had found herself and was happy again."

Closely akin to the dream state is the phenomenon known as astral projection or out-of-body experience, which often takes place during the hours of slumber or during the hypnogogic state; that point between consciousness and unconsciousness just prior to deep sleep, often referred to as the Alpha state. During the OOBE the individual is often able to travel through time and space to other planes of existence or to other points in time and space to see once again events that took place, not only in other physical lives, but during a time between incarnations.

Anne Pickering of Cedar Rapids, Iowa, gives us a view of such an event that happened to her:

"I have had many out-of-body experiences since I was a small child. All occurred in a sleep/dream state, in color and concerning happy situations. Some of them pertain to reincarnation.

"An out-of-body experience when I was fourteen or fifteen left me overwhelmed with feelings of love. Until that time I was without conception of love, but listening to the man in my dreams, who was later to become my 'teacher,' I knew I loved him with all my heart, always had, always would. Such a strange sensation for me! He stood by a fireplace, his face in the shadows, smoking a pipe whose aroma was pleasant to me. He explained he was going away to study, but would return to teach me many things. I awoke weeping, awed by my emotions and the experience.

"The same young man returned, as he'd said he would, when I was in my late twenties or early thirties. He took me to a huge, marble-like building where we were greeted by a white-robed, white-haired, white-bearded attendant. My teacher, or guide, spoke to him, and the attendant left, only to return with a huge book which he put into my hands. The pages were brittle, some papyrus, some paper. The bottom of the book had a hard cover, but the top had no cover because my life was unfinished. I tried to read the pages but could not penetrate a mistiness that hung over them. At another word from my guide, the man gently removed the book from my hands and, bowing, walked from the room. Again, I awoke in wonderment.

"On another occasion, I asked my teacher if the incarnating spirit inspired the conception of a body for it, or if the body 'brought the spirit to be born into it' by being already formed when the spirit was ready. I then saw myself as a young female spirit whose loved one was being prepared for a new life on earth. I was grieved at being alone again, although I realized I was also to be reincarnated soon to be with him. Three masters, or doctors, brought him to me in infant form; I was allowed to kiss him farewell. Then, all smiles, they simply held the form over the woman whose body already showed the pregnancy. They released him and he slid, comatose, as if magnetized, into the body."

Dr. McHenry, through hypnosis, has regressed numerous clients to the point of their death in a previous life, and he has then taken the entity through the "limbo" stage to the point of selecting another physical body and to the actual rebirth into the present life.

"I have found those who have died without knowledge of spiritual advancement or spiritual training. I find many times that these entities were in limbo. They knew nothing from the time they died. They may recall the final clinging to the body, and then they seem eventually to lose interest in that body. They may have existed in such a state for 100 to 150 years. Then suddenly, wham! Here they are being born again. In this case they are usually already a child by the time I can pick them up.

"Those who have been metaphysically trained in past lifetimes are totally aware of the passing, of the state right after passing, and on through to a period of time spent on different levels, some in the philosopher plane, some in other planes, depending on the soul evolution of that entity.

"When the time comes for their rebirth, they are aware of the approaching event and they even make their choices. They find themselves observing the mother-to-be. She's already pregnant, but they are not there yet in the fetus. I wish more people understood this, because of the legal discourses going on right now about abortion and when a fetus is actually a human being.

"I have found several instances where the child was actually several days old before the entity or soul entered the body permanently. There are also cases where the entity moved into the fetus before birth, but for some reason moved out again, then went back later. It seems the entity is free until such time as the child is actually born into the physical world.

"I remember one very rare case where a lady was in quite a bit of confusion as to which of two women was actually her mother. One person claimed to be her mother, yet she always had a gnawing feeling that her mother was really the other woman. This lady was in her forties, but she had held this feeling all of her life and could never understand why.

"Finally, she came to me for a regression to find out if she could hit this early area in her life and settle the problem once and for all. It proved to be very interesting. I was able to drop her consciousness back into a spiritual consciousness before her current birth. Then we brought her foward in time. In truth, she had been born to the woman she felt was her mother, but she had died after a few months and was then reborn to the second woman—her present mother.

"Since that happened, about two years ago, this woman has gone ahead in her career, and has been very successful in the field of metaphysics. She works in dream interpretation and in social work, where she has been quite successful. Before the regression, she found that people did not accept her well, and she was too aggressive in trying to overcome this problem. She has a better sense of balance, a sense of well-being, and a sense of stability, which make it possible for her to function better in a middle-of-the path matter."

Today we see people of all ages escaping the fast pace and confusion of modern living and finding peace in their own ways. Some seek a certain serenity away from the big cities, escaping to small towns and rural areas. Many well-educated young men and women are living in communes; businessmen have given up high-paying executive positions with giant corporations and retire early to rusticate or find tranquility in the village life. Why? Because they are trying to find that evasive element called "peace." And in finding their inner peace, they may eventually understand their spiritual nature better.

We are into a New Age. Concepts advanced by the principle of reincarnation and Karma are a very viable part of it, for today as never before in the history of man, we are learning to benefit from past lives. This is helping us to make this life, this incarnation, the one that will break the continual cycle of rebirth and eventually lead us to the higher realms of spiritual development.

# Chapter 15

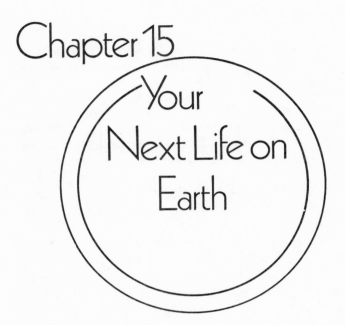

## Your Next Life on Earth

Ann Fisher believes that people do live after death. "We have a physical and a spiritual body, and after death our physical body dies and our spiritual body goes to the Fourth Dimension, as we may call it, or to the spirit realms. There is a choice whether we want to stay there and progress or to come back to another physical life, in which we choose our parents and lifestyle in order to complete something that we did not fulfill in the past. All of us have the opportunity to return to continue the cycles of life and rebirth."

"As a final thought," the Frosts suggest, "beware the

Catch-22 of reincarnation. That is, if you *expect* to be reincarnated at the human level again after this present experience, you probably *will* be. For thoughts are real."

Anne Pickering relates:

"On one occasion, my teacher drew a design, explaining that with each incarnation the two lines changed until they ultimately merged, with all memories open to us, those of body and spirit lives. When this occurs it is not necessary that we return to earth unless we should desire to work here for others' progression. We are, of course, born unto a great purpose and are responsible for accomplishing it.

"These experiences allowed me to understand Jesus' words about intentions being as great as the actual act. Purify the thoughts as much as possible! There is no place *there* for unpleasant thought power. There is much beauty, love, and joy about those who dwell there that meet our longings, but we need to prepare ourselves for these things. The evolution of spiritual self is, it would seem, a practicality of many lifetimes."

Dr. Leichtman says:

"The matter of selecting the details of subsequent incarnations is something which can be comprehended only as an event carried out from the level of an immortal and all-knowing essence which can afford to take a rather impersonal perspective about the experiences that a future personality may have to endure. The choices and plans are worked out with the assistance of more experienced beings and in accordance with laws which govern right human relationships. Then, in accordance with the opportunities available to select the optimal body, sex, home conditions, environment, etc., more specific plans are made for a subsequent incarnation. Some reflection on this is necessary to grasp the fact that the inner immortal essence is quite willing to bargain for more than the personality is able to bear sometimes—or at least bear with equanimity! Without that understanding, reincarnation will not make much sense to the personality which will tend to rationalize that the concepts of reincarnation are unfair."

The basic purpose of reincarnation is to balance our past experiences so as to perfect the life and wisdom of our immortal essence, a point agreed upon by most Reincarnationists. This means that for the most part there is the general purpose of cultivating some special set of human talents, strengthening some set of personality traits, and compensating for previous weaknesses or indiscretions. The errors to be corrected are, therefore, errors both of omission and of commission. The talents to be perfected are any of the wide range of human potential.

Dr. Leichtman further points out that there are also purposes that transcend the *individual* concern. Whether we like it or not, we also participate in humanity as a whole and are subject to participating in the more far-reaching purposes of humanity to build a perfected civilization. Easier to comprehend are the instances in which an individual, as part of his life plan, has taken on the responsibility of assisting another individual, such as a future spouse or child or even the parent. A few have teaching as their major purpose, but this is rare. According to Dr. Leichtman:

"I stress these fundamental concepts about the purpose of reincarnation to conspicuously avoid the common misconception of thinking that the purpose of reincarnation is to stop coming back. No longer having to return to physical life is a side effect of having perfected one's human nature or character. And it is said that persons in such a position are the very ones who then volunteer to return, as they are then best able to help others.

"Fundamental to the entire concept of reincarnation is the fact that there is an immortal essence in each human being.

This is a higher level of consciousness which is able to extract the good, the bad, and the indifferent experiences from each incarnation. These experiences and qualities of character which have been expressed in an incarnation are then added to the sum total of all previous experiences. Where certain deficiencies and imbalances still exist, general plans are made for adding new talent, elements of character, and humane expression through subsequent experiences while in a physical body."

Nancy French once told me:

"I chose the parents I did because I knew they were people I could control!

"This could sound to some people as if it had some malice in it, but it isn't that way at all. If there are certain things a person wants to do, is it not wise to choose parents or an environment which will present the least amount of friction? What is one to gain by choosing a family that's going to resist? When I say 'control,' I mean a lack of resistance to the individual's goals and intentions. On many occasions my body would argue with me that it was more work than could be done in a single lifetime, and I would say to my body, 'You're quite right; it *is* more than can be done in one lifetime, but that's alright because all of it isn't your responsibility.' In other words, just so much will be done within the confines of one body lifetime, and after that, another body will be 'picked up' and the work will be continued.

"In *Highest State of Consciousness,* John White refers to the few who are brave enough to be frontiersmen: the ones who 'take the ball' even when there is not a game to be played, yet make a game to be played—psychic research, frontiers of the mind, or whatever. But no single individual can go too far beyond the collective consciousness of the rest of mankind, or contact is lost. If we, as frontiersmen, want to go very far, there still has to be contact with the 'mainland.' If there isn't, things that are needed on a shared basis are lost. One doesn't let civilization hold him down, but neither does one let down civilization!"

The question remains, however: to what kind of civilization can we expect to come back?

Dr. Shealy may have found the answer in yet another facet of hypnosis:

"I have also tried *progression* under hypnosis several times, and had it tried once on myself. I took a friend of mine, Jerry, into very deep amnesiac hypnosis and asked him to project into the future and give me his impressions. Interestingly, even though he is not at all attuned to the psychic world, what he reported is going to be happening in the next twenty years was essentially what the vast majority of psychics have been saying for the past several years. Now, where did Jerry pick this up? Well, you could say it was from me, telepathically, and it's entirely possible that I projected what I had heard from psychics.

"Some of the things he said were a bit more specific and time-oriented than I would know, and he did give some things that I had never heard of. And he did a progression on me right after that, and I had very good visions of things evolving.

"For instance, I saw my own death scene. It was intensely vivid. This is, of course, negative programming, for you can say if I die at that age that I have been programmed to do so because I saw that vision. I have discussed this with several psychics who say that everything you see clairvoyantly is a probability, not absolutely essential fact.

"After that, we went back a few years in the progression and I saw myself with my wife standing up on a mountain in Flagstaff, Arizona, looking at the Pacific Ocean! The year was 1990. Interestingly, some part near San Francisco was still there.

"I felt that my son was in San Francisco at the time of my death. I had a picture of a piece of the country being covered by water, but a big gulf—another Gulf of Mexico—was there, going out past the San Francisco area. All I can say is that I feel strongly that we are likely to have certain catastrophic events in the next twenty years.

"I saw war in the Middle East sometime before 1988. The United States will be involved in this devastating war! Both Jerry and I saw world-wide catastrophic events, partly natural and partly due to war, reducing the population of the Earth by huge percentages. We saw a return to a much more agrarian and simple life because of the breakdown in mechanization. I have had this feeling for a long time that we must prepare to be able to sustain ourselves."

"Do you think it will be an 'Atlantis' type thing all over again?" I asked Dr. Shealy. "Lost civilizations, and perhaps a return to a primitive existence?"

"I don't think we'll go back that far—to primitive times," Dr. Shealy said. "I saw us building a hospital after the catastrophe. I felt that I was somewhere in the Southwest. If I saw the area, I would know it immediately. I don't think we'll go back too far—I think we'll reduce to a life style more like about a century ago.

"Barring something else happening to prevent it, tremendous numbers of people will starve to death, and because of this we will be reduced to a significant alteration of lifestyle. Of course, you've also got to say that we are paving the way for this thing, which in itself may help to bring it about."

I had to agree with Dr. Shealy. The predictions from many sources—psychics, Amerindian Medicine people, and economists—may, in reality, be putting bad "vibes" into the ether. Maybe a little more positive thinking along these lines would help. But in a sense, such progressions are nothing more than what psychics regularly do when predicting future events, or what those ancient seers accomplished when they wrote prophecies which accurately foretold of World Wars I and II and events beyond the year 2000.

Although one cannot vouch for the validity of progression any more than he can the absolute truth in regression, it might be interesting to speculate as to what might be accomplished from a practical standpoint should such be possible. If Dr. Norman Shealy was able to foretell the time of his own demise from this current incarnation, what would happen if we were to progress, not merely to the end of this life, but well beyond into what could be a future incarnation of the Earth plane of existence?

Regardless of theories to the contrary, we are accustomed to thinking of time in a linear sense, so for the sake of clarity based on the acceptable methods of the present, let us assume that time is indeed composed of past, present, and future. Let us further assume that those who view the past and present are akin to a high-flying airplane, from where the pilot can see great distances ahead as well as behind—into the future as well as the past.

Now, in our giant psychic 747 we are able to view our next incarnation just ahead in the realms of time and space. What do we see? For one thing, we see a new personality that is greatly influenced by the life we are living today, just as we today are the sum total of all our incarnations of the past. We can see objectively, or feel subjectively, what this future human being is experiencing in that future life. We can experience his loves and hates, his successes and failures. We can see what he is doing with his life, based on the Karmas he is obligated to work out. It is, in a way, a similar experience to that of Scrooge when he was given a glimpse of what would be if he did not correct his erring ways.

We may not be able to change the past, and we today find ourselves working out Karmas which resulted from past actions, good and bad. It may be too late to do anything about the past, other than to atone for it in some way, but is it too late to change the future? Hardly, because in a linear sense, the future has not yet arrived.

Wanda Sue Parrott told me of her experiences in progression wherein she saw herself in a future life as a blind mutant named Aldena Krois:

"When I made the motion picture *Death Is Not the End,* a study of a future life called '75 I.T.,' I discovered that in the hypnotic trance, my receptor brain was capable of attuning with intelligence that seemed to reach far back into human history and to reach just as easily into future lives.

"I do not really know from where I got the information, nor do I know if I will really come to Earth again as Aldena Krois, the blind mutant living under a unified world government whose headquarters are in Africa. But *I* will never return to this earth to live again, nor have I ever lived before! This is my personal belief, based on this explanation: Wanda Sue Parrott, the body that is known by this name, will never come again, because when this body has served its time, it will devolve back into elements that will become fish or grass food! Nor has it ever been here before in this exact form.

"Now, the inner spiritual self—call it soul, personality, inner person, or whatever other name denotes the Vital Life Force— has probably been here multiple times and will probably be here again. Reincarnation, to me, is easiest understood if you imagine yourself sitting on a cloud. Below you are several thousand human bodies, in the shape of drinking glasses. Some are like champagne glasses, others like beer mugs and yet others like pitchers! The air is like a vast sea of water. It spills down into the cups. It fills them up.

"These vessels are not fulfilling their function until they are filled up with this invisible essence. So it is with living things; they are not fulfilling their function until what I call the Godspell spills into them and sparks them to life. That is, a human body is planted on the earth. It breaks down into simple elements, such as nitrogen. A plant's roots grow in the soil containing the once-human elements. Certain root hairs absorb parts of the humus that was once human. The plant absorbs nutrients in this manner and new leaves grow. When the plant matures, a flower forms. It dries up, leaving a seed. The seed falls into the soil. The next spring the seed sprouts and becomes a near-duplicate of the plant that absorbed the cells that once were part of a human body.

"As long as the Godspell, or call it soul force, spills through your body, you are *you*. Your body has a name by which it is identified, but the intangible spiritual part of yourself is often mistaken for the body's name. The inner you is invisible, so it is easy to identify yourself solely with the body.

"While the Vital Life Force remains in my body, nature (or God) is conserving. That is, my cells are being conserved in this one multi-celled conscious unit called Wanda Sue Parrott, which is a female body with a nonsexual intelligence, or spirit.

"Every seven years we grow a complete set of new body cells, science tells us. Is this not a simple but eloquent statement about the veracity of reincarnation? I believe it is. I believe it is also miraculous, for we do not change personality or identity every seven years although we do change cells!

"Ten years ago I was known as Wanda Sue Parrott. Since then I have changed cells one and a half times! Another way of stating it is to say, 'I have changed my body once this past decade, and am halfway into a second body.'

"When spirit and flesh coexist, the flesh makes possible the spirit energy's conversion, while the spirit makes possible the flesh's conservation. At some point, however, in each body's cellular continuity a time comes when the spirit separates from the mass cell structure known as 'you.' When one dies, I believe the physical and nonphysical parts of self separate. When the Vital Life Force separates from this body, the process of conversion will occur: that is, it will all break down so conservation can result again when energy assumes a new form. When this happens to me, Wanda Sue Parrott's identifying cells will undergo devolution, returning to natural chemical elements of the earth. I should be very open about realizing the cells that now compose the fingers that typed this manuscript may very well someday integrate themselves into the blooms of a rose that springs forth from the place where my remains are planted in the soil.

"This is purely a demonstration of physical law, but what about the nonphysical levels of being? Death—or that period of 'waiting to be born again' on a spiritual energy level—might just be the other side of life. The physical body's growth from life through transition may be considered a finite demonstration of the conservation principle. The spiritual element, or Vital Life Force, might be undergoing its period of conservation while out of the body; that is, it may remain as energy-not-in-motion while residing purely in cosmic energy realms.

"Understanding this principle makes it easy for me to accept the spectre of death. In fact, I seldom worry about death. My greatest problems have involved figuring out what to do with myself while living here on earth, as Wanda Sue!

"The term reincarnation—which means one's spiritual self or soul personality coming to dwell in another body of flesh—generally is considered mystical, and therefore impossible to resolve as a scientific theory. I believe that the nonphysical part, the quintessence of being, my Vital Life Force, will return to whence it came. I should not care to try labeling my spirit with a name, but if all matter is always recycling, either in a state of conservation or conversion, and if matter is a mirror of natural law as it functions throughout the Cosmos, it would follow that if the Godspell spills once into a life form, it would spill again into a life form when natural law ordained this be done.

"Perhaps my inner spiritual soul personality will then take on the body of Aldena Krois; but if this does happen, it won't be Wanda Sue Parrott making her return through reincarnation. It will be part of the Godspell spilling down, energizing a newborn body and giving birth to a girl named Aldena Krois, who, too, will live only one lifetime.

"I believe in infinite intelligence, and I believe mortal man can contact this wonderful source of wisdom. We do not do it physically, but by attunement on spiritual levels. Our brains are receptors, or repositories of impressions received from raw energy. We are capable of cognizing these impressions through the wonderful cerebral faculty we humans possess called self-awareness or Ego.

"I believe that as we trust more and more in the spiritual part of ourselves, the greater will be our awareness of the Godspell spilling through our physical bodies, and the more vast will be our mental contacts with intelligence, which is never physical, be it in the body or on the 'other side.' "

We do not really understand how closely knit the past, present, and future may be, for our concepts and realities are limited by our lack of overall knowledge of such matters. We are conditioned throughout life to believe that time runs from seconds to years to centuries. We know that the American Civil War ended a specific number of years ago, because we have records and calendars which are based on linear time. We know that on a particular day it is May and that it is the second day of May because we were conditioned to believe this, and it is universally accepted by the civilized world around us. We know that it is 2:30 in the afternoon, because as children we were taught to tell time. But is linear time absolute? Or is it just man-made like the car we drive, the political party we vote for, or the house in which we live?

Perhaps, in the truer sense, we are still living in that lifetime a thousand years ago, and are already living in that future lifetime a thousand years hence. In that case, we are a part of the Eternal Now, and the changes we make today have already changed that personality we may be tomorrow.

While it would be only normal to want to perpetuate the pleasant aspects of life throughout eternity, most of us would not care to have reruns of the negative sides of life. So in a sense we control the whole Karmic principle by avoiding the pitfalls of another future life in correcting them here and now, thus preventing them from ever becoming a part of our personal reality.

Let us for a moment imagine ourselves under hypnosis, and instead of regressing to the past, we are progressing to the future. We see the personality that we are to be one hundred years from now. This personality is learning the lesson of what poor health means. He is just recovering from major surgery that resulted from living with disregard for common sense health practices. Careless living has caught up with this future person. "But wait," you say, "I do not live recklessly in this life. I eat regularly, get plenty of rest, and my drinking habits are quite moderate. How could I build up a Karmic condition that would lead to such a future life?"

Is it possible that since you *do* enjoy good health this time around, you may have developed a rather smug outlook and a lack of empathy for those less fortunate? Are you perhaps even critical of your less disciplined brothers? Perhaps a bit condemning? Perhaps you do not really *appreciate* your own good health, taking it for granted. What then have you learned of the value of good health? Appreciate it now, so you do not have to lose it in a future life in order to *learn* to appreciate it then.

This is but one small example of how progression could be used in a pragmatic sense, by teaching us what pitfalls to avoid now in order to aid the evolution of that future lifetime.

The implications concerning the advantages of progression might be limitless. Each of us knows areas in our present personal life that can stand improvement. With a little thought, we can figure out for ourselves what corrections can be made now to offset the unnecessary failures of the next and subsequent incarnations.

What talents do you have? Music, art, writing, public speaking? How are you using them? If you have certain dormant abilities which were handed down from past lives, but which you are not currently using, they will atrophy and eventually become lost. Use them now, if only as a hobby or avocation. Do not waste them, for by the next lifetime you may no longer have them, even for your own pleasure. Continue to keep an active interest in those talents, and perhaps a century from now you can be a master painter or a concert pianist or the author of the novel the world has been waiting for for a hundred years.

We cannot say with conviction that progression can be accurate, for only the future itself can prove the future. But since we can establish a reasonable amount of truth which can be documented through regression, who is to say that we do not hold in our hands today the power to change the future for the better, through knowledge, limited as it may be, of the future.

# INDEX